CONNECTIONS

Everyone Happens for a Reason

Jerry Davich and Dennis Berlien

Copyright © 2009 by First Connections LLC

Published by First Connections LLC, 2008, P.O. Box 649, Portage, Indiana, 46368

Printed in the United States of America

First Edition: May 2009

ISBN-10: 0-9820859-0-7
ISBN-13: 978-0-9820859-0-5
Library of Congress Control Number: 2008910128

Book design: Greg Russell

Book editor: Ron Kenner

Cover photo credit: Susan Sorensen (The connected hands are of author Dennis Berlien and his son, Boston.)

Text photos credit: Cherie Davich, and iStock images.

Several stories and columns within this book were originally published, in some form, in the *Post-Tribune Newspaper of Northwest Indiana*. Copyright 2006, 2007, and 2008. Reprinted with permission. The authors are grateful for the newspaper's generosity.

For more information, marketing or promotional materials, requests for speaking engagements or workshops, or to stock our book for sales, visit www.connectionsbook.com or mail us at Connections Book, P.O. Box 649, Portage, Indiana, 46368.

Thank you to the "wholly" trinity
of personal connections in my life
— my mother, Nancy, my wife,
Cherie, and my daughter, Ashley
— the strongest links in my life's
chain.

— Jerry Davich
November, 2008

Thank you to my parents for their
unwavering faith and belief in
everything I did; my wife, the
most important connection in my
life; and my children, our greatest
blessings.

— Dennis Berlien
November, 2008

Connections
illustrates a
renewed awareness
of human links
in your chain of life.

CONNECTIONS

Table of Contents

"Only connect."
— *English novelist E.M. Forster*

Laws of Connections

In May, 2004, two cousins, Dennis Berlien and Jerry Davich, after being apart for nearly two decades, stayed up late one night pondering their lives — past, present, and future.

With wives and kids long asleep, we revealed shades of ourselves and shared a mutual epiphany about the key "connections" we experienced with others in our lives — both the obvious and the ones to which we are oblivious — including a series of seemingly random connections that ultimately renewed our relationship.

While discussing in Dennis' Las Vegas home the direction and meaning of our lives, Jerry lamented how he missed too many key connections in his life: Not spending enough time with his two children while they were young … a possible job he let slip through his grasp … an acquaintance he mistakenly ignored … a distant relative who drifted away. He simply had too many "missed connections," he told Dennis.

Our conversation led to pondering why: Fear of failure? Fear of success? Ignorance? Arrogance? Bad timing? Lack of belief? Lack of luck?

We concluded that such key connections act as precursors not only in our lives but in everyone's life. These connections, we realized, ultimately determine our successes and failures — in love and contentment, in business and beliefs, from womb to tomb.

Connections, the *concept*, was born from that late-night conversation. We first introduced this concept to family and friends, then to others in our daily orbits. We later explored it with dozens of other people, then hundreds, then thousands, over the next four years, asking them about *their* connections and missed connections.

Connections, the book, is the culmination of those conversations. Its intent is to illustrate, as we have learned, that it's not always what you know but also *who* you know and how you connect with them. Along the way we will transform the popular adage, "Everything happens for a reason" into insights that better reflect what we've learned from all these people.

Thus, the Laws of Connection:

• "Every*ONE* happens for a reason" in our life.

• The quality of our life depends on the quality of our human connections.

• Missed connections typically lead to regrets.

• It's never too late to create new, meaningful connections.

How to Connect With This Book

Before you begin reading this book and embarking on the journey of connecting — and reconnecting — with others in your life, we first want to suggest how to use this bound compilation of insights, information, and real-life stories.

For starters, *Connections* isn't simply a book. It's *your* book. This isn't a schmaltzy marketing tool. It's a matter of practicality. We designed this book not only to be read but also to be used as your journal, a way for you to retain spontaneous thoughts on paper and then to reconnect them days, weeks, even years later. Consider this book a barometer of where you stand today regarding connections in your life, and a dated baseline for comparisons in the future.

Both of us, Jerry and Dennis, have read countless books in our lives, and we habitually write notes, quotes and thoughts on the inside pages. Trouble is, we've noticed there is usually very little space, if any, on book pages to write our endless notes, quotes and thoughts. We're often forced to squeeze in an observation here or a question there, an idea here or recollection there, wherever we find empty space.

The result is usually a haphazard hodgepodge of undecipherable doodles, scrawled ramblings and laughable shorthand that we can never make sense of a few days — let alone a few months or years — later. Sound familiar with any of your books?

Our intent here is to spark personal connections in your life, to serve as a conduit of connections in your world, and to help you reflect on the people in your past, present, and future. (Yes, future connections. We'll explain this later.)

Our suggestion: When you read something in this book that sparks either a memory or idea or connection, write it down, immediately, on the blank margins we've provided every few pages. We've titled these *empty margins*, "Connect Your Thoughts," and we hope by the time you've finished this book that these margins are filled with connected thoughts — Your thoughts.

There's no need to search for those typically hard-to-find empty spaces on inside pages, or in the preface or epilogue (as we've personally and repeatedly done in other books). Remember, this book isn't about us and our connections, or even other people's connections we're using to illustrate our points. No, it's about you. Any thoughts you have while reading in this book about connections should be immediately and, hopefully, easily chronicled. This way you can get back to reading instead of turning the book every which way to scrawl down your own notes, quotes and thoughts.

At the end of each chapter we've provided even more empty space for additional notes, personal summaries, or thoughtful reflection on what we hope becomes your favorite new slogan, "Everyone happens for a reason." We strongly suggest you transform these empty pages into a makeshift journal, crammed with any thoughts that pop into your head while reading this book.

To help spark this brainstorming process, we pose self-reflective questions for you to contemplate. For example, *"Have any of your missed connections turned into regrets that have simply not faded away?"*

We also end certain chapters with a list of "Action Items," designed to prompt or motivate you to make any changes you feel are needed. These are simply suggestions to ignite more personal decisions in your particular situation. For example, *"Which freshly penned thoughts in the margins of this book can lead to new connections?"*

All of these questions — both inside this book and on our Web site — are to provoke not only answers from you but, hopefully, will generate more questions about your life, your world, your connections. Why? Because this isn't merely *any* book, it's **your** book. For life.

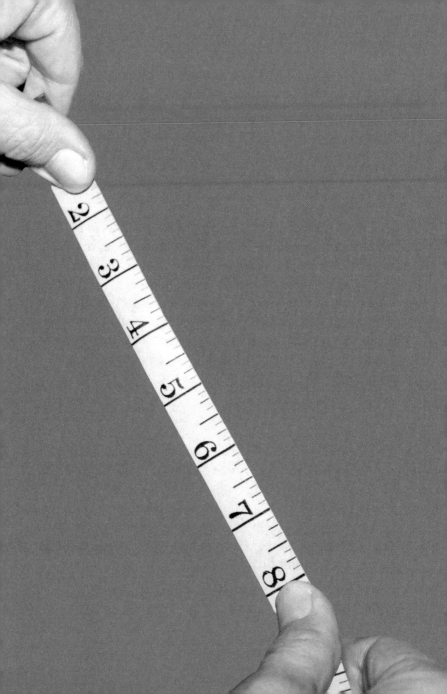

"Chance favors the prepared mind."
— *Louis Pasteur*

Measuring Life's Connections

Walt and Marlene met in the first grade after their families moved next door to each other on a one-block street in Upper New York. As childhood chums, both came from broken homes, celebrated First Communion together and attended the same school. As a dreamy young girl, Marlene told herself, "I'm going to marry him someday."

As teenagers, they faded away from each other. Walt quit school to make a living out of town and Marlene focused on her classroom studies. One day, while Walt visited their hometown, the two accidentally bumped into each other at the movie theater. "Write me sometime," she sheepishly suggested. He did just that, as often as possible. They kept in touch and met regularly, again, as often as possible.

At age eighteen, Walt confided to his mother: "Mom, I want to marry Marlene." His mother asked, "Are you sure? It's for a very long time." Walt didn't blink. "I'm sure." With a $30 engagement ring, he marched into the home of his seventeen-year-old sweetheart, who was doing her homework on the sofa. Walt proposed on the spot. Marlene didn't blink. On the spot, she said, "Yes!". Marlene's uncle 'gave her away' at the wedding. Walt and Marlene eventually moved to the construction yards at the southern tip of Lake Michigan where Walt could put his chiseled body and massive hands to work.

They raised two sons. There they began fixing and fusing her poor engagement ring, which often lived down to its $30 price tag. There, they began investing in their 401(k). Not the kind with direct deposits and compounded interest but the plan that stashes away priceless moments and compounded memories. Let's call it an emotional 401(k), one with life's special moments squirreled away into memory vaults for decades. As the years peel away, these 'direct-deposit' moments draw interest, priceless moments either banked in the back of your mind, or stashed away through photos, videos, or scrapbooks. Think of it as a 401(k) for the soul.

Walt and Marlene were expert bankers when it came to such life investments. When their sons were young, they loaded up their camper and trekked the country; actually, all fifty states. Once Walt drove 27 straight hours while his wife and boys slept. He didn't mind it a bit. As the couple got older, they eventually visited more than 35 countries on six continents. They vacationed around the world, as often as possible, usually on a shoestring budget or as part of a tour group. At every port of stay, they deposited their 401(k) memories like sea-side tourists, digging up souvenir shells along a newfound beachfront. Over time their modest home became filled with such souvenirs — a chunk from the Rock of Gibraltar, Atlantic Ocean sand, a bottle of Japanese Saki, tundra from the Rocky Mountains, ash from Mount St. Helens. You get the picture.

Today the couple has been married more than a half century. Their 401(k) of the soul is brimming. You can find Walt using his workman's hands gently picking a guitar on the front porch or penning mushy love notes, displayed on the kitchen refrigerator, to Marlene: "Life is a journey. Thanks for taking it with me. Love always, Walter."

Walt's journey in life taught him many lessons, but none more valuable than connecting with a profound appreciation for each moment, each day, each excursion into the unknown. To prove his point, Walt sat down on his living room recliner and pulled out an imaginary measuring tape from his pocket. He counted off his age in imaginary inches — 10, 20, 50, 60, finally 71 — and he pinched the tape at that spot, watching as he let several feet of invisible years fall to the floor.

"Do you see that?" Walt asked, staring down at the tape on the carpeting. "That's gone in my life." Then he looked at the short remaining inches of time left on the imaginary tape. "This," he said, pinching the spot, "this is what I have left to live. We have no regrets, but I know some people do."

We share Walt and Marlene's story — and his imaginary

Connect your thoughts

measuring tape — to remind you that regardless of how young you are, how old you are, or how many life souvenirs have been deposited into *your* 401(k), those inches of life's past remain on the floor. You can only learn from them. You'll never get them back.

Today — right now, at this moment while you are reading this book — is where your personal tape measure gets pinched and your life gets measured. Go ahead and pull out your imaginary tape measure and pinch it at your age today. Now look to the floor. Are you staring at a wreckage of regrets? Are there missed connections there? Missed opportunities? Looking back, what could you have done to take advantage of those missed connections? What should you have done? Either way, as Walt wisely noted, that time is gone. It's history. It's in your rearview mirror. And that's OK.

Now, look up and stare at the remaining "inches" of your life on that imaginary tape measure. How many inches — years — are left? Go ahead, play pretend with us and guess. Five years? Ten years? Fifty years? Who knows, right? Regardless, those remaining inches are filled with potential connections to make your life more contented, more meaningful, and more successful. We want to help you ponder these connections, discover them, and ultimately utilize them. What we don't want is for you to pull out Walt's imaginary tape measure in five, ten or twenty years, pinch it again, and look back at even more missed connections. That would be a travesty. That would be the most important connection to miss in your life: Connecting with yourself.

Now is the time to imagine your life with new connections, with renewed connections, and with a new outlook toward every single connection.

Today is the perfect opportunity to change your "shift-in-time perspective," a term coined decades ago to define the same critical point in all our lives; the one that typically takes place during our middle-aged years when we stop viewing our life from birth to today and start viewing it from today to our life's end.

Go ahead and ask yourself: Am I connected?

Of course you are. Everyone has connections in his or her life — to family, friends, business associates, loved ones. To one's past, future, and one's spirituality. Yet from what we learned talking to thousands of people across the country, too many of us have lost, forgotten, or fractured all too many connections in our lives. Others have let key connections slip through their grasp without ever knowing of their existence.

Now can be the time to adopt a fresh awareness of those connections in your life — past, present and future — and

Connect your thoughts

how these unions can transform your perception, your life, and your world.

Think of it. Why do people endlessly seek companionship, togetherness, and a sense of belonging in our society. Or any society, for that matter? The answer: Human connections.

This primal need — not only timely, but timeless — is our original wireless connection with face to face value and eye to eye contact. No need for Blackberry batteries, a strong cell phone signal, or a laptop computer. The new buzzword of the fast-paced twenty-first century is *high-tech* "interconnectivity." Just look at all the cyber-social networks such as Facebook, MySpace, LinkedIn, and Twitter. Not to mention the millions of "conversations" taking place via email, instant messaging, and in the blogosphere at any given moment.

But at what cost? From what we can tell, the price is *human* interconnectivity.

Along the way, many of us have become oblivious to this eons-old primitive need. While mass-messaging is easier than ever, key personal connections have slipped through our grasp for unexplainable reasons. These disconnects often cost us a coveted career, a revered relationship, an elusive enlightenment. Sometimes we look back wondering what went wrong more than what went right.

It's these pivotal connections that reveal who we are and how we got to where we are in life. But more importantly — with your tape measure getting pinched today — you can begin capitalizing on future connections you may have otherwise missed.

We already pinched our tape measure, but this book isn't about us. It's about you. We will disclose ours to help illustrate certain points, but it's not about *our* connections. It's about *your* connections, about some you've taken advantage of, and others that have taken advantage of you, and about the difference between the two. This book also looks at dozens of other people who realized, in hindsight, they too had key connections in their lives — everyone from your average next door neighbor to Dr. Mehmet Oz, of "Oprah" fame (who disclosed to us his key connection in life, at age seven).

You also will hear from a boy named Tyler who turned tragedy into triumph through his newfound connections; from Janice, who regrettably wedded a career instead of a mate; and from Jon, who pedaled across the country only to find himself. There's also, Phil, whose genuine "miracle" confirmed a Catholic saint; and there's Sandy, whose sickly baby had more to do with this book than you might think. On and on it goes — connection after connection.

Everyone, we've learned, has such associations in their

Connect your thoughts

life. Everyone also has several missed connections, more typically called regrets. To illuminate the importance of these, it merely took prodding by us and reflection by others. *Their* connections can link you to *your* connections. We're not saying that every incident, accident or circumstance will be a vital connection in your life serving as some sort of tell-tale sign or mystical coincidence. And we're not offering pie-in-the-sky promises about metaphysical meanderings that circle themselves with psycho-babble. No, we're simply suggesting the discovery — or rediscovery — of all of our crucial connections — from love and contentment to business and beliefs. From our first breath to our last wish.

While also realizing our own missed connections and being more aware of our future connections, we believe that few if any have pondered this concept more than we have these past several years. We've talked with so many people, surveyed their key connections and missed connections, and studied their responses. We discovered that yes, everyone happens for a reason — yet too often we don't take advantage of it. We don't recognize, for example, a possible job promotion through a health club buddy, or a possible love interest through a church friend, or a little girl who needs her Daddy's attention.

We learned that many of us don't realize, scrutinize, or actualize these obvious yet seemingly oblivious human connections — and that it costs us in one way or another.

So, ask yourself again, "Am I connected? Am I connected enough?" We can't answer these questions. Only you can. Other more universal questions to ask include:

• Are we fully aware of all our human connections?
• Do we recognize people who can help motivate and inspire us?
• Do we tell them what we want, what we need, and what we seek?
• Do we utilize these connections on a regular basis?
• Do we appreciate them, nurture them, and protect them?
• Do we weld together every possible human link in our life's chain of relationships?
• And, just as importantly, do we forgive ourselves for those missed connections of our past?

Through *Connections*, we hope you find a greater insight into the same two words of wisdom echoed by every spiritual leader who walked this planet: Know thyself.

Through *Connections*, we hope you will see fresh opportunities in familiar faces, while not allowing another link in your chain to become rusted, broken, or invisible.

Through *Connections*, we also hope you'll never look at a measuring tape the same way again, and that you begin investing in the 401(k) of your soul.

Turn the page and let's get connected.

Connect your thoughts

*"The area where we are the greatest
is the area in which we inspire,
encourage and connect with
another human being."*
— *Maya Angelou*

Getting Connected

Carolyn is in heaven on this weekday morning. It's here, in a church, where the 47-year-old woman donates her time each week to cook soup, bake desserts, and serve bottomless smiles. It's here where the church offers "Soup and Serenity" to anyone hungry, lonely, or both. It's here where Carolyn chooses to connect with people — first as strangers, then as friends.

On this day she stands in a circle with other soup kitchen volunteers and prays. On this day, a record 107 guests flood through the door. The joint is hopping. On this day, like every other week, she sits behind a piano, waves to a regular guest named Edith, and plays her weekly request, "Somewhere My Love."

Carolyn learned to play by ear years ago and still misses a note occasionally. No one minds. She doesn't play the most flawlessly, only the most thoughtfully. She takes a sip of her canned Fresca soda from the piano top, cheerfully waves to another guest, and then tears into "Stardust," a favorite for the older crowd.

Another soup kitchen volunteer wanders over to the piano. Bad news: The homemade chicken noodle and split pea soups are running out fast. "Uh-oh," Carolyn says, flipping through her song book. "I better play something upbeat." In a few minutes, she will receive a gift signifying rebirth, renewal and resilience. She has no clue it's on its way.

On the very same weekday afternoon, in another corner of the world, Keith carries an Easter basket into a hospital near his home. Sporting a uniform and badge, the 44-year-old auxiliary policeman smiles like a Boy Scout earning his first pin.

Keith strolls into the hospital's main lobby and charms the older ladies behind the information desk with gift Beanie Babies. They giggle like schoolgirls. "Which floor is pediatrics?" he asks politely. "Third floor," he's told. Off he goes. He strides from the elevator and approaches the pediatrics ward where sick children are stuck indoors on this sunny day.

"Hi, I'm Keith with Kards 4 Kids," he tells two women behind the window. "I have an Easter basket for the children." The homemade Easter basket is filled with plastic eggs, bunnies, candy, Beanie Babies, and sports cards. "Please pass it out as you see fit," he tells the women. "And Happy Easter!"

Keith strolls back to his pickup truck. Four hospitals down, he says to himself, "One to go." One last Easter basket awaits him for another pediatric ward of sick children, kids he'll never meet in person. It doesn't matter. As long as they get the cards and the gifts. That's why he called off work on this day. That's why he made the baskets the night before. That's why he collects items for the baskets all year long.

Carolyn and Keith don't know each other, have never met, and probably don't have much in common. Except for one thing. On this particular day, among other days in the year, they both chose to do something for others. No strings attached. No questions asked. No hidden agendas. Just... to connect, in its purest form.

She leans toward comforting older folks. He leans toward comforting little kids. This might help explain things.

On March 29, 2001, Carolyn, a wife, mother of two girls, and a registered nurse, was diagnosed with a very rare cancer of the appendix. (For the record, it's called "poorly differentiated signet ring adenocarcinoma.") That pivotal day, she asked her oncologist point-blank, "What's my prognosis?" The oncologist said only two words: "Very poor."

Connect your thoughts

In that instant, the bottom fell out of Carolyn's life. Experts told her there was no hope. But she didn't listen. She researched the best specialists, the best treatment, the best hope. Somehow, she escaped death. Later, her cancer lowered its ugly head into remission. Since then, her personal prognosis was a new, purposeful life.

She created a Web site and one-woman help-center for other survivors of her type of cancer. She's literally helped save and extend lives across the globe. She also volunteers for Meals on Wheels. She organizes collections for troops overseas. She plays piano at nursing homes and, as you learned earlier, at a church where she's not even a member.

Since her diagnosis on that fateful day, "I've watched flowers bloom in the spring five more times, celebrated five more of my kids' birthdays and five more Christmases," she writes on her Web site. In short, she experienced a rebirth — a resurrection, if you will.

Keith's motivation and inspiration came at age 14, when he was involved in a traffic accident. The pickup truck he rode in spun out of control. Its driver, his father, was impaled by the steering column. He later died. In the hospital, the young teenager stayed overnight far from home.

Thirty years later, Keith still hasn't forgotten how it felt.

In 1997, he began a 'Kards 4 Kids' program, collecting donated sports and trading cards and delivering them to kids, usually in hospitals. It's a national effort that he adopted, typically making his rounds every Christmas, Halloween, and Easter. He believes it eases the pain for bored, lonely kids stuck in hospitals. He believes it helps him connect with these faceless kids. But he also believes it connects him with a 14-year-old boy who once was stuck in a strange hospital after an unforgettable accident.

As Keith delivers his last gift basket, Carolyn plays piano to a room full of strangers-turned-friends. During a popular song, a flower delivery person walks in and places a beautiful bouquet on Carolyn's piano. She curiously stares at it while she plays. Finally, after playing Jim Croce's "I Got a Name," she leans up, smells the bouquet, and reads the name on the card.

The flowers are from her best friend, Rose. The card reads, "I'm so proud of you." Rose knew that exactly six years ago on this day Carolyn was diagnosed with a deadly cancer. Yet Carolyn is still here to celebrate it, despite what several experts first told her. Carolyn knows this, too. Her emotions can't stay in remission any longer, not even while

Connect your thoughts

playing piano in public. A single tear runs down her left cheek. She sits back down, tickles the ivories some more, and joyfully celebrates the sixth birthday of her new life.

We introduce you to Carolyn and Keith because they both illustrate the word "connecting." They prove it's an action word. Connecting with others is something you do, not something you say you're going to do. (*To view a photo of Carolyn, visit our Web site at www.connectionsbook. com.*)

No one on this planet knew this more than Felice Leonardo Buscaglia, a.k.a. "the love doctor" to his admirers, including us. Dr. Leo was a self-help author and professor who offered the class Love 101 at the University of Southern California in the early '70s.

He also wrote more than a dozen or so best-selling books which sold millions of copies in twenty different languages. And he once defined "love" as a journey by which we connect ourselves intricately with other travelers in the paths of life. Love can be expressed with the same fervor toward a romantic partner or for a pasta dinner, Dr. Leo was fond of saying.

Dr. Leo died in 1998 of a heart attack at age seventy-four, but not before connecting with tens of thousands of other people through his signature style — hugs. That's right, Dr. Leo was the world's best hugger. And probably its most famous hugger. Tight, lengthy, meaningful hugs, like from your grandmother after a long time apart.

Dr. Leo also gave the most wonderful lectures, although he never called it "lecturing." He always called it "sharing." Well, Dr. Leo *shared* the most delicious stories about his youth, offering eternal pearls of wisdom from his tight-knit Italian immigrant family and his beloved "Mama" and "Papa." "Every night at the dinner table, each of us children had to tell Mama and Papa one thing we learned that day," Dr. Leo would say as he heated up, taking off his suit jacket and loosening his tie. "And you better believe that we either learned something new that day or we didn't eat."

"Sometimes," Dr. Leo would quip, "I had to peek at an encyclopedia after school."

Dr. Leo often told the story of a woman driving her car around a bend on a mountain. As the woman made the blind turn, a car passed closely by her and the driver yelled "Cow, cow!" The woman, offended and insulted, countered by waving her fists out the window and returning the remark: "You're a horse's ass, too!" Then she turned the bend in the road, and hit a cow.

Dr. Leo would laugh with his audience, wipe the sweat from his brow, and continue on his way of showing us that sometimes trust, faith and good-natured fun-poking is allowed, even encouraged.

Connect your thoughts

But Dr. Leo made a name for himself by hugging everyone after he ended his motivational "sharing," a habit that continued up to his last speech. He always said his Mama taught him how to hug early in life and he never forgot how good it felt. Dr. Leo ended all of his sharing speeches with hugs for everyone, as long as you didn't mind waiting in line. At each lecture, hundreds of adoring fans didn't mind one bit waiting for their hug from the "love doctor." And it didn't cost them — or him — a dime.

You don't need to be a professor to realize that not all connections have to be dramatic epiphanies, like those Carolyn experienced, or accompanied by life or death consequences, like those Keith discovered. Some are as subtle as a sunrise. Some as simple as a hug. The trick is to be more aware of them when they arise. This is exactly what Beverly, a.k.a. the "Happy Birthday Lady," learned at the tender age of seventy.

On this day, Beverly leaned back in her rocking chair, double-checked her detailed notebook, and dialed a phone number. Sporting comfy sweatpants, old gym shoes, and a nervous smile, the retired teacher didn't waste any time.

"Hi Anita, it's Bev, are you ready?" she asked. "OK, here we go." Beverly cleared her throat and in her best church-choir voice, began singing into the phone. "Happy biiiiiirrrrrrthday to youuuuuuu, happy biiiiiiirrrrrrthday to you, happy biiiiiiirrrrrrthday dear Aniiiiitaaaaa, happy biiirrrthday to you. and many mooooore, and good ones, and healthy ones, too."

"Happy birthday honey," Beverly tells Anita, before closing her notebook and exhaling a smile.

For the previous two years, Beverly has been singing the most popular song in the English language to hundreds of people across the country.

"The lord got me into all this, sort of sneaky like," explains Beverly from the rocking easy chair in her living room. What she means, she's been singing in the church choir since childhood, along with the glee club and other choirs. Then one day she was asked to sing "Happy Birthday" to a church friend. So.... It was her first solo ever. Her first connection to a new identity, too.

One "Happy Birthday" led to another, and then twenty, then two hundred, and it's now up to one thousand and counting. It got to be such an endeavor that Beverly, who taught for more than thirty years, now uses a thick notebook to chronicle who she called and who she's going to call.

As a retired math teacher, her "Birthday List" notebook is very detailed, including how to correctly pronounce everyone's name, and her own set of codes, such as "05/07 LM" for "May 7, left a message," and "ch" for "church

Connect your thoughts

member."

Since starting this in 2006, she's also had quite a few "repeat birthdays," requested from birthday boys and girls of every age who want her to call them back every year. So, of course, she does.

"Who doesn't like being sung the Happy Birthday song on their special day?" she asks. Exactly. That's why Beverly's notebook is filling up fast with names of friends, loved ones, and even strangers she meets at the grocery store or bank.

Her busiest day so far has squeezed in seven "Happy Birthday" phone calls, and her busiest month is August. She's not sure why August is so busy, but she's guessing because it comes, ahem, nine months after December, when the cold weather gets couples to "snuggle" more.

Many listeners ask her to purposely call their voice mails so they can save her singing message for others to hear.

"I stay pretty busy," says Beverly, who never married and has no children. "But I love doing this. It makes me feel a part of their lives, even if it's just for a day— their birthday!"

Sure, Beverly could have ignored her fellow churchgoer's initial suggestion to sing that very first "Happy Birthday" to a friend. She also could have chalked it up as a one-time thing. But she didn't. She chose to connect, and she acted on it.

This is why it's important to not let such opportunities slip through our grasp. Once they do, it's hard to get them back. It's like trying to squeeze toothpaste back into its tube, or replacing fallen leaves onto a tree. Remember, missed connections can eventually turn into jagged, tough-to-swallow regrets. And haven't we had enough of those in our lives?

Consider this chapter your official notice and reminder to look for every possible connection every day. At first, since "connections" are not part of your daily vocabulary, this may not come naturally — yet. Initially it didn't come easy for us, either, or for the other people we talked to for this book. But now we see connections everywhere — at home, at work, in the grocery store aisle, on vacation, in our past, and also in our future.

Each time, we're gently reminded to be more aware of connections, regardless of where we're at or what we're doing. And you will too. We understand that there is no "Connections 101" class in high school or college. But, if it helps, remember the "three Rs." Not reading, writing, and 'rithmetic, but recharge, refocus, and rethink. Recharge your emotional batteries. Refocus your attention to possible daily connections. And rethink any missed connections.

It also takes action. Here are a few tips:

Connect your thoughts

Set aside a few minutes in your day to zone out, day-dream, or meditate on your life and its direction.

Contemplate the people in your daily life who may become new friends, loyal confidants, or career builders. Or, do you unknowingly and habitually close the doors on people who could help you?

You don't need any special props, additional purchases or ruby red slippers to tap into your connections. All you need is to tap into yourself and your own Emerald City experiences, while remembering our First Law of Connection, "Everyone happens for a reason."

Pick a convenient time to think of connections. Maybe early in the morning while the rest of your family sleeps. Or late at night after everyone else has gone to bed. Maybe it's in the shower, or while driving to work each day on autopilot.

Cruising on autopilot is a dangerous way to direct your life and its destination. Have you been doing this for years, even decades, unaware of your connective surroundings and human landscape? Have you been coasting blankly through life, winding up and down the road of regrets while wondering what happened to those weeks, months, or years in between? Has your groove turned into a rut without you even knowing it?

It's so easy for us to sometimes feel like Sisyphus, the Greek mythological character who was condemned by the gods to roll a huge boulder up a steep hill — only to watch it roll down the other side; and then have to repeat this throughout eternity.

All of us have our boulders in life, even if it's our daily

grind. Right? If so, maybe it's time to take a cue from Keith, Carolyn, Dr. Leo, and Beverly. Time to put your boulder to the side for a moment and consider how you may want to connect with others. It doesn't have to be through an Easter basket, playing piano, a lifetime of hugs, or singing "Happy Birthday to You." Getting connected can be through whatever gift you want to give, to others and to yourself.

Connect your thoughts

*"Life without connections
is death without a witness."*
— Adapted Spanish proverb

Missed Connections

As though facing the edge of a cliff, retirement, Janice had no idea what waited beyond.

The long-time federal official, now a one-woman encyclopedia on public health issues, would soon be leaving her hurried and harried office for the proverbial life of leisure.

In less than a month from when we talked to her, Janice would no longer be wearing her familiar blue uniform with yellow stripes on the shoulders, similar to that of ranking military officers. In less than a month she'd no longer be dedicating herself to informing citizens about myriad public health issues. In less than a month, she'd be forced to focus not on her job but on herself, a major change for her and millions of work-minded baby boomers in her current situation.

Asked about her future, she says softly, "I'm not sure what I will be doing."

As with a great many others, a significant part of Janice's social identity came from who she was at work and how she made a daily dollar. Think of it: One of the initial questions we ask when just meeting someone is, "So, what do you do?"

Sound familiar? We never reply by saying, "Well, I can do crossword puzzles." Or "I can do fifty push-ups in a row." Or "I'm a father of three." No, we usually reply how we go about making a legal buck in the world. Whether deserving or not, on target or not, it's typically how we first define ourselves,

Janice was asked whether she had any second thoughts after so many decades of being focused on her *job* and not on her *life*. After pondering the not unexpected question, she replies, "No, not really." But, seconds later, before she jumped off that retirement cliff without looking back, she stopped and pondered the question again: Hmmmm, any second thoughts? "You know," she says pensively, "I do have *one*."

Yeah, what is it?" she is asked. Was it that she felt bad about not finding a miraculous vaccine for AIDS, cancer, or multiple sclerosis? Or that she wished she had more years on the job to build her retirement savings? Or that she didn't have a clear-cut plan in the works for her upcoming golden years?

"No," Janice replies, shaking her head, admitting now that her second thoughts had nothing to do with her job.

This was the precise moment when Janice experienced the epiphany of a "missed connection" in her now middle-aged life. This is when she found out, as with her job, a missed connection can be just as powerful as a cherished connection. This is when she realized that a missed connection can oh-so-easily crystallize into a life-long regret. Missed connections have a way of linking themselves to us for years, even decades, like a ball and chain around our hopes, dreams, and future.

"I regret not saying 'Yes' to the last man who asked me to marry him," Janice says, pausing to hear her own words sink in.

As Janice can attest, we're a society that often values *what* we are more than we are. And it sometimes takes the realization of a missed connection — a human connection — to understand this everyday phenomenon. Some missed connections slip through our fingers like invisible gusts of wind while we're busy making other plans. Others whip past us camouflaged by our fears, ignorance, or arrogance.

Actually, when we stumbled onto the importance of connections, it was the notion of failed connections that began the conversation. Regrets, unlike other more idyllic memo-

How many "missed connections" do you have in your life?

ries, have a way of burrowing into our hearts and minds, a sharp pain never fading entirely away, year after year, decade after decade.

We, too, have had to swallow some painful regrets in our lives — as husbands, as young fathers, and as business professionals. Here is one example, from Jerry, illustrating how regrets don't fade away like memories but often linger on like a chronic illness.

It began as an innocent act of thievery, prompted by a longing for her Daddy. Jerry's daughter was a toddler at the time who didn't want to wave good-bye again.

It happened just before Jerry was to leave for yet another night on the town. As a twenty-something husband and father he was searching for what he thought was missing in his life. Sadly, that search didn't always include his little girl. So, in her first act of rebellion, his naïve yet hopeful daughter grabbed her father's car keys. And she hid them, figuring that it would surely stop her Daddy from leaving home again.

Silly girl. Silly girl.

At that time, Jerry didn't know his little girl was the culprit who swiped his keys. He figured he misplaced them himself. But he was running late for excitement that night and getting angry about his predicament. Those keys helped him escape his own home, he figured, and his life was passing him by. So, out of sheer desperation and stupidity, he picked an argument with his wife.

Not surprisingly, she's his ex-wife today. What they fought about is of little consequence now.

Maybe it had to do with Jerry's missing a rock concert

that night. Or maybe it symbolized something more, much more. Whatever, Jerry angrily grabbed another set of car keys and stormed out of the house, not thinking twice about the two children he was leaving behind — again. Years later, it finally dawned on him that his daughter's act of larceny was simply an attempt to keep her Daddy home.

Silly girl. Silly girl.

More than a decade after that incident, Jerry stumbled across an old home movie of himself with his very young daughter and son. Out of curiosity, he watched it with his daughter, who is now twenty-four. In the videotape, the three of them were home alone, dancing, jumping, singing and screaming as rock music bounced off the walls. A video camcorder recorded the occasion.

It was like watching a stranger in a strange land. "Who is that guy?" Jerry silently asked himself. The tape showed a tiny girl raising her arms toward her father. She obviously craved his attention. The father sees her. The father whisks her off the floor, twirls her playfully and sets her down. Then the father resumes his raucous antics.

The little girl sobs a bit. Her eyes follow her father around the room. She waits to be picked up again.

Silly girl. Silly girl.

Connect your thoughts

Fast forward a few years from that videotaped evidence. The young girl was now a young woman, and her eyes had other destinations besides her thirty-something father. Hugs didn't come with such a tight grip those days. Kisses were fewer and farther in between.

In hindsight, Jerry learned that regrets were merely memories that wouldn't fade away. They also come with sharper-resolution illustrations — making them more vivid and more unforgettable. It's not that he was a young father who didn't hold his little girl, or hug her, or tend to her needs. He did. Just not nearly enough.

But those missed hugs — at that tender age, with such immediacy — have a way of never materializing again, he realized years later. And, he has since realized all too well, these moments of regrets remain frozen in time. For some people, like Jerry, they're even frozen on videotape.

Years later, when Jerry's daughter turned sixteen she received her driver's license. That day she was ecstatic over the possibilities, including the sweet freedom to drive herself wherever she pleased without having to ask her father for a lift any longer. She didn't have to rely as much on him, plain and simple. But that day, Jerry was just beginning to realize exactly what he was losing. That day, he began to understand how, unlike a memory, a regret doesn't fade away so easily. That day, without knowing it, Jerry experienced one of his first missed connections.

Even after his daughter received her driver's license, Jerry desperately tried to come up with a plan: Maybe, he told himself, if he hid his daughter's car keys … No, it was too late. Much too late for such a childish act.

Silly Dad. Silly Dad.

Does Jerry's lingering regret ring a bell in your life? Do you see how powerful missed connections can be? How they can linger in your life no matter how busy you try to stay, how much money you make, or how many consumer goods you buy?

Regardless of our situation or a dozen other factors that separate us from each other on a daily basis, we all have some regrets or missed connections. And regardless of all the high-tech communication concoctions in our ever-shrinking world, there is no vaccine against regrets.

Janice learned this, and so have we. Realizing that missed connections are a universal — and oh-so-human — trait is the key to identifying them and correcting them. It doesn't

Have any of your missed connections turned into regrets that have simply not faded away?

matter who you are, where you live, how much you earn, or what faith you profess.

What we've learned first and foremost during our research about *missed connections* is that they often lead to loneliness in some form. This country is brimming with more than three hundred million people. And although we've never been as "connected" to each other — by email, text message, instant message, cell phones, Blackberries, cyberspace chat rooms, you name it — we're firm believers that loneliness has reached epidemic proportions.

So with all these opportunities to communicate and connect with each other, we're not *really* very connected. Not where it matters most. Actually, we're becoming increasingly more socially isolated. More alone. More disconnected. That's right — *disconnected*!

We see it everywhere — Do you see it too? — whether it's early in the morning with familiar-faced breakfast diners or late at night with same-stool barflies. We see it in nursing homes, grocery stores, Internet chat rooms. We even see it in the workplace with employees who routinely come in early, stick around late, and linger on a regular basis. Does this subtle behavior — this scenario of loneliness — seem familiar to you?

It's not merely us, the authors, who see such disconnectedness across the country. The United States Census Bureau has observed it, too. The federal agency's latest census figures reveal that one-fourth of all American households are comprised of just one person. That's it. One! Compare that with figures of a half-century ago when only one in ten households included just one person. Our point: More people today are living alone; some willingly and happily. Others, not so much. And, clearly, more people today are living lonely — lacking human connections.

A prime illustration of this phenomenon was revealed when we dined at a restaurant and sat across from a man with an obvious lack of human connections in his life. (By the way, once you begin seeing the world through a Connections outlook, the haves and have-not's stand out in stark contrast to each other.) The old man most likely had struggled with several missed connections in his life — He stood out like a funeral without any guests.

The old man stared at us for quite a few seconds, clearly violating society's five-second rule of acknowledgment among strangers.

You know the rule — when you first see someone in public you're allowed up to five seconds to glance their way, nod, smile or ignore them, and then return to whatever you were doing.

Well, the old man stared at us for at least fifteen seconds. He sported a huge wool coat, a toothless grin, and a set of

Connect your thoughts

tired eyes that fixated on every single patron in the eatery at some point, including us.

After we settled into our booth we returned the old man's silent greeting, nodded, smiled, and opened our menus. After we ordered, we couldn't help but notice that the old man had all the telltale signs of loneliness, our society's way-too-quiet epidemic.

First off, all the waitresses seemed to know him, his name, and his all-too-familiar lines and jokes. Secondly, he ate very slowly, repeatedly looking around the restaurant for eye contact from everyone and anyone. He longed for a conversation. He yearned for interaction. He craved to connect with someone. Anyone.

Finally, after eating, he pulled out dollar bills as wrinkled as his hands, yet waited patiently for one last bit of dialogue with anyone before going home — alone. Minutes later, his waitress hustled past again. He motioned for her to come over. When she did, he grabbed her hand and pulled her close, whispering something in her ear.

"Oh, you take care now," she told him, politely pulling away.

"Good night, honey," he told her.

"Good night," she replied.

As the old man stood up, he looked like an old suit on a dusty hanger in the back of a forgotten closet. After he left, we thought to ourselves that the old man's momentary grasp of the waitress's hand may have been his only human touch of the day. Who could blame him for reaching out for companionship? We all do that in one way or another. It's as human as childbirth. It's the most primitive means of connecting with others. And it's slipping away from our high-tech, fast-paced 21st century grasp, just as that young waitress pulled away from that old man.

Here is another example illustrating the obvious lack of connections in our lives. In 2006, the American Sociological Review published a major study showing that the average American gets through life with only two close friends — yes, just two friends whom they confide in and with whom they share intimate details about their life. A similar study from twenty years earlier showed we had, on average, three such friends. In other words, we're losing friends. That's right, we're losing *intimate* connections.

But it gets worse. Nearly one quarter of those surveyed for this updated study said they have no such friends or

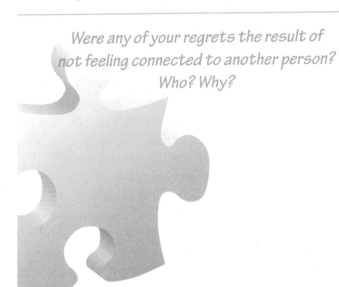

*Were any of your regrets the result of
not feeling connected to another person?
Who? Why?*

confidants at all. None. Zero. Not one. Talk about loneliness. Most of these individuals would have to talk about the issue of loneliness to themselves!

Imagine having no one with whom to share your joy, your aches, your laughs, your pains. The study, "Social Isolation in America: Changes in Core Discussion Networks Over Two Decades," illustrates Americans' social landscape as a "densely connected ... set of ties slowly closing in on itself, becoming smaller, more tightly interconnected."

Yet the study also found that while our new technology allows us to connect over larger distances, it diminishes our need to create a safety net. These ties also lead to civic engagement and local political action."

The lack of these outside-the-home connections taps into a broader social phenomenon known as "bowling alone," from the book of that title by Robert D. Putnam in 2000. His ground-breaking research and book showed how people today have become "disconnected" (his word, not ours) from each other, and how we now belong to fewer clubs, know less about our neighbors, and meet less with friends.

And, although more Americans than ever are bowling for recreation these days, they're not rolling strikes in bowling leagues. They're rolling gutter balls by themselves.

We're so disconnected from each other, Putnam says, that we're even bowling alone. How sad is that?

In many ways we have "Disneyfied" the nature of relationships, offering only the storefront façade of personal connections, but without the goods inside. This reminds us of the 1970s song, "Big Yellow Taxi," by Joni Mitchell: "They took all the trees, put 'em in a tree museum. And they charged the people a dollar and a half just to see 'em." Doesn't that sound more familiar today than ever?

Not only does loneliness disconnect us from each other, according to another eye-opening study from Rush University Medical Center in Chicago, it also disconnects us from ourselves. The 2007 study, published in the Archives of General Psychiatry, found that being lonely in old age can double the risk of getting Alzheimer's disease. That's right. Even though previous studies have proved that social isolation is directly associated with higher risks of dementia and cognitive decline, Robert S. Wilson and other Rush University researchers showed how being disconnected from other humans plays a huge role in our mental health, at any age.

Other research studies clearly show that behind-the-scenes loneliness should be considered a serious, life-threatening ailment, increasing the risks of such well-known conditions as chronic stress, depression, and heart disease.

"This underscores the importance of being *connected* to

Connect your thoughts

others," Wilson told media when the study was released. "Humans are very social creatures. We need healthy interactions with others to maintain our health."

According to the new book "Happiness: Unlocking the Mysteries of Psychological Wealth" by father and son authors Ed Diener and Robert Biswas-Diener, happiness includes creating, developing, and nurturing relationships — human connections.

"The pursuit of material riches is not worthwhile if it means giving up relationships," write the authors, who have devoted their life's work to the field. It's not just adults who are lacking relationships these days. Children today also are also experiencing "a lack of connectedness," according to The Commission on Children at Risk, an independent initiative of the YMCA, Dartmouth University, and the Institute for American Values.

Its report, "Hardwired to Connect," warns of an ongoing crisis involving more children with mental problems and emotional distress from feeling disconnected in their young lives. We see this in our own kids' lives. For instance, when Dennis' five-year-old son, Boston, zones out his surroundings for hours at a time while watching television. Regardless of age, meaningful human interactions are simply an interconnectedness that appears to be in our DNA. Many of us live and die without ever really connecting to each other, or anyone at all. Take, for example, Eleanor Rigby and Father McKenzie.

If you recall, Eleanor "picks up the rice in the church where a wedding has been… lives in a dream. Waits at the window, wearing the face that she keeps in a jar by the door… who is it for?" And, if you recall, Father McKenzie can be found "writing the words of a sermon that no one will hear… no one comes near. Look at him working. Darning his socks in the night when there's nobody there… what does he care?"

Sound familiar? Let us refresh your memory. Try singing this musical refrain: "All the lonely people, where do they all come from? All the lonely people, where do they all belong?"

That's right, it's the timeless ballad about loneliness from the Beatles. Remember its ending? "Eleanor Rigby died in the church and was buried along with her name… nobody came. Father McKenzie, wiping the dirt from his hands as he walks from the grave… no one was saved." (Feel free to

Do you feel you don't deserve, or weren't smart enough, rich enough, educated enough, or something else, preventing you from making these connections?

curse us at will if you keep humming this song the rest of the day and can't get it out of your head.)

Yes, indeed, "all the lonely people," where do they all come from? Well, we believe they come from being disconnected from each other. We believe they come from being disconnected from society. More to the point, we believe they come from missed connections, as Susan can attest.

Susan is a beautiful 37-year-old woman with short blond hair, an infectious smile, and a heart of gold. But, using the 20/20 vision of hindsight, she dearly regrets the missed connections in her life, especially with her father.

"My father and I had so much in common," she told us. "But he just could not, and would not, see it. He was blinded by anger, his religious beliefs, and the conviction that women were created only to be wives and mothers, always under a man's thumb."

"My personality would not allow for this," she says. She asked us to remind parents not make the same mistake with their children that her father made with her. "Find out who your children are, what their interests are, and what they might thrive on if given a little help," she suggests. "My life is less than it could have been if someone had just believed in me. If someone, anyone, could have seen past the cute little blonde girl."

Unfortunately, Susan has not been able to "get past" her childhood and grow as an adult, she says. She is still searching for that fatherly figure to love her, support her, and defend her, unconditionally, no questions asked. "I'm still looking for that missed connection," she sighs.

Now you should be more aware of missed connections and the regrets they're attached to, like shackles on a condemned prisoner. Now that you are more aware of them, you can be more aware of how to avoid missing these connections, and also how to reconnect with connections from your past. It's never too late to return to your life's chalkboard, erase your failed drawings, and start new ones. Remember, you're the engineer here, not the two of us. We're merely consultants on your project.

The new plan is to think of your missed, or misfired, connections as potential lessons.

And your coaching plan is threefold:

•Reconnect with missed connections.

•Be more aware of every new connection that comes your way.

•Reach out and *make* new connections in your life.

It can be as simple as a smile or as complex as a new business proposal. It can be as rewarding as a new relationship, or as a chance to earn a living doing what you enjoy.

One way to begin practicing these lessons is by heeding the words of singer-songwriter John Prine from his poetic

Connect your thoughts

ballad to older people, 'Hello in There'":

"Ya' know that old trees just grow stronger, and old rivers grow wilder ev'ry day. Old people just grow lonesome, waiting for someone to say, 'Hello in there, hello'.

His advice?

"So if you're walking down the street sometime, and spot some hollow ancient eyes, please don't just pass 'em by and stare, as if you didn't care. Say, "Hello in there, hello."

Easier said than done? Of course.

In some ways, it comes down to your attitude about regrets, and living in the past.

Country singer Willie Nelson once sang, "Regret is just a memory written on my brow, and there's nothing I can do about it now."

We disagree. We prefer to harmonize with this anonymous quote, popularized by college basketball coaching legend John Wooden: "Regrets are simply disappointments that you couldn't, or wouldn't, correct."

Wouldn't you rather begin looking more through your life's front windshield and less in your rearview mirror? We would. More often than not, as people within this book can attest, you'll find opportunities in your windshield and regrets in your rearview mirror. So which pane of perspective do you peer through each day?

We also want to point out another common thread from our research: All of us need to start paying attention to what we may have become oblivious to through the years. We heard this from the majority of people we spoke with, and in September, 2007, we experienced it first-hand.

Dennis visited Jerry's home in northwest Indiana to complete this book project. Dennis' plane from Las Vegas landed at Chicago's Midway Airport, which is surrounded by residential neighborhoods, light industry, and several railroad tracks.

While driving through Chicago, Dennis pointed out something Jerry had become oblivious to after decades of battling traffic in that city: Trains. That's right, trains. Being an out-of-towner from Las Vegas, Dennis made an off-the-cuff "Mork from Ork" observation about all the trains that crisscross Chicago. Dennis' city, he noted, doesn't have nearly the amount of trains.

*What can be done today to reconnect
with your missed connections?
What can be done next week? Next month?*

(Don't Google it! Mork from the planet Ork was the hilarious alien character portrayed by comedian/actor Robin Williams in the late1970s TV sci-fi sitcom "Mork and Mindy." Mork often viewed life here on Earth with an alien's curiosity, seeing things with a fresh outlook. All of us could use such Mork from Ork self-observations about our lives, making the oblivious obvious again, and seeing things with the curiosity of, well, an alien.)

Anyway, Dennis' keen observation about all the trains in Chicago reminded us of what so many others have told us: Familiarity and repetition often puts us to sleep in our own lives. This prompted us to try to see our lives and daily orbits with the eyes and outlook of an alien, or in Dennis' case, an out-of-towner. You too should try becoming an out-of-towner in your own life, as a tool to discover, and rediscover, connections in your public, personal, and professional circles.

By the way, Robin Williams happened to portray another fictional character who perfectly illustrates how to see life from a fresh perspective. He played an idealistic and inspiring English school teacher named John Keating in the 1989 film, "Dead Poets Society," teaching his impressionable male students how to "Carpe Diem" —seize the day. He did this, in part, by having them one day stand atop their classroom desks, simply to help them see things differently than their usual, ho-hum perspective. It worked. At the end of the film, when Mr. Keating eventually gets kicked out of the rigid boys academy, a few of his like-minded pupils paid him the highest honor by again standing on their desks and declaring one by one, "Oh, captain, my captain," showing that they would forever remember his lesson. Is this a lesson all of us should heed as we re-educate ourselves about identifying new or missed connections? We think so.

A final illustration involves, oddly enough, trains, and again looking at our life from an out-of-towner's perspective. The following paraphrased parable has been credited to American author, satirist, and all-time anti-hero Kurt Vonnegut, regarding how all of us perceive — or misperceive — reality. It goes something like this: Imagine you're riding inside an enclosed boxcar of a speeding train through

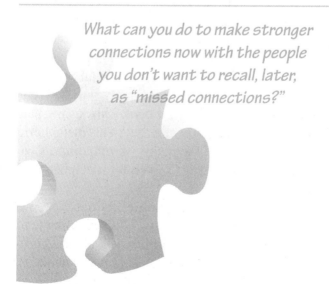

What can you do to make stronger connections now with the people you don't want to recall, later, as "missed connections?"

a foreign land. The boxcar has no windows, no openings, and is completely dark inside. The train is hurtling down the tracks, shaking you about, heading for an unknown destination … somewhere.

In the rear of the darkened boxcar, near the floor, you spot a pencil-thin ray of light sneaking in from the outside world. You try to find the source of this light beam, and you trace it to a tiny crack in the sidewall of the boxcar. It captivates you. You kneel down to get a better look at that tiny hole. You bend over and peek into the light, through the hole, stopping the beam with your curiosity.

Through this tiniest of holes, you catch a glimpse of the blurry landscape that the train hurtles through, but only barely. You can make out only distant images as the train passes them at a high speed. This is your only view, your only perception of where you're at and where you're going. You look back into your dark boxcar and wonder if you were better off not knowing anything at all, rather than the limited landscape through that hole. It's all you have to make sense of the outside world. Simply put, it's your only portal to any life beyond your own. This, as the parable goes, equals our perception of reality. This metaphoric boxcar hole is how little of the reality surrounding us we can actually see, let alone try to interpret, decipher, and understand.

With all the things going on in our life, our universe, our soul — simultaneously and constantly — it's impossible to absorb, let alone interpret, the enormity of it all, the complexity of it all, the reality of it all. It's simply our nature to try to fill in these blanks, to make the unknown known, to connect the dots in our often paint-by-number lives.

It's also our nature to transform meaningless and incomplete information into meaningful and fuller understanding, even if our minds conjure irrational connections to make sense of things. This is why we see, for example, clouds that create recognizable images, and why we see the images of Jesus Christ in a stain on a wall. It's for us to connect our dots of human relationships. We're wired this way. It's our nature. And we're sharing this with you to illustrate that our world is infinitely bigger than we think.

If you've been kneeling at your boxcar's tiny hole, struggling to distinguish your world, we're here to help you expand it. We're here to help you connect the dots in that station-to-station interpretation of your life. We're here to help you find your boxcar's sliding door so you can swing it open and see what you've been missing. We believe your boxcar's destination, and every stop in between is all about connections — and missed connections. We simply don't want you to have the same regrets we have, or those that were made by all the people we talked to for this book project.

Now let's start getting more connected.

Connect your thoughts

*"It's never too late to become
who you might have been."*
— *English novelist George Eliot*

Connecting With Yourself

Jon, a 32-year-old Emergency Medical Technician, took his one big shot in life. He chased his childhood dream, faced his adult fears, and connected with himself all at the same time in the spring of 2007. That's when he hit the road for a 2,500-mile solo bicycle trek from his Indiana home to Los Angeles. That's when he made the decision to apply as an LA police officer, his dream job. And that's when he began realizing the power of new connections along the way.

But several speed bumps were in his path: He trained on the only bike he owned, an old Raleigh women's road bike with cracks in the tires and rust on the spokes, costing $25 from a resale shop; He was overweight and woefully out of shape. And he's a former epileptic who could have a seizure at any time on the road, alone.

"All of that doesn't matter," he said before he left for L.A. "It's now or never." So Jon hit the road, with pie-in-the-sky plans of camping at state and national parks across the country, and providing Internet updates at wi-fi cafes and libraries along the way. He knew he was taking his once-in-a-lifetime shot.

"My family and friends say I'm crazy," he said, "but I really think I can do this." After word got out about Jon's cross-country trek, he heard from fellow epileptics who offered to buy him a new bike, no cost too high, no questions asked. He heard from a woman whose father died years ago and whose bike gathered dust without him. He heard from a recently paralyzed bicyclist who now had a bike to spare. And he heard from a man attacked by a lower-body infection who bought a bike but never rode it. The list went on and on.

"This isn't just about me and my dreams anymore," Jon said. "It's about all the people who have been so kind and supportive of me."

But there was one particular stranger, Bob, a 67-year-old retiree with several peculiar connections to Jon, not to mention that both men are five-foot, seven-inches tall. Bob offered Jon his customized Trek 1200 bike, modified for a similar cross-country trek he planned — but never made — a few years earlier. Bob's bike was loaded with extras: A "granny gear" to ride up steep hills; a light all-aluminum chassis; a small tool set and spare tire under the seat; Kevlar belted tires to avoid a flat; an air pump if needed; even a mini-computer to tabulate miles and speed. He also offered any accessories Jon needed, including a waterproof sleeping bag, a high-tech backpack, a portable heater, fanny packs, and a pocket journal and pen.

Bob, unexpectedly, even offered to take time off from his part-time consultant job to drive alongside Jon and provide road support with his GPS-equipped van. Bob knew what Jon was facing, after similar experiences as an endurance runner in his younger days, and once running 100 miles in the Utah mountains. Bob told Jon, flat out, that he too was once "young and crazy enough" to try such a cross-country trek. And that he planned on doing so after he retired, but … we'll get to that in a minute.

From a distance, it may appear that Bob was the sole giver here and Jon the sole receiver, right? But it was a two-way street, with a landscape of odd coincidences along the way. You see, the reason Bob never made that cross-country trek is that his wife, Chloe, was diagnosed with cancer before he could even try it. He retired instead to care for her.

As her cancer spread, she was transported by the same ambulance service where Jon was an EMT, from one hospital to another in a last-ditch effort to save her life. We'd like to tell you that this ambulance trek saved her life. But it didn't. Chloe died in 2005.

Since then, Bob has been grieving and, admittedly, depressed at times. "Jon has indirectly made me get out of bed, off the sofa, and plan for another adventure in life," Bob said. "Jon has done more for me than I have done for Jon. If he makes it or not, we both are winners."

Either way, Bob was convinced that Jon's dream had

Connect your thoughts

rescued him, too. He told Jon, "What you are doing has given me renewed hope that I can get back on a bike and fulfill my dream, too." But wait, there was one last coincidence, or connection, between the two men. Bob knew he was doing the right thing all along by helping Jon, but especially after he read when Jon's trek would begin. The date was Aug. 18. Bob's wife, Chloe, died two years earlier on that day.

The phone call arrived in Jerry's voice mail box at 6:36 a.m. that day, a Saturday morning. It was from Jon, who already had a misgiving about his once-in-a-lifetime cross-country charity bike trek. Oh, he was still leaving for L.A. In fact, he was almost in Illinois when he called Jerry.

No, his only misgiving was not inviting Bob to ride in a support van along the 2,500-mile route. Jon also just learned, from the road, that Bob's wife died on his launch date.

"This man literally enabled my dream," Jon said. "Who am I to say he can't have his dream?"

Jon called Bob and invited him to ride alongside him. Bob accepted the invitation. He immediately cleared his calendar, including two part-time jobs he held. Two days later, he emailed us, saying, "Thank God Jon has given me his blessing to be his support vehicle. Later that afternoon, another email from Bob read simply, "California or Bust." By 6 p.m. that day, he had gone into the Wild West yonder. A few days later the two men were already in Kansas, as

Jon biked about 100 miles a day in hot and humid conditions. By that point he already had six flat tires and two numb hands, and he couldn't get enough sunscreen or Gatorade.

But, as Jon chased a new career and Bob took a sabbatical from his, the two men began a friendship on the road. They also began making new connections along the way, including a helpful police sheriff, and a campground host named Judy who generously fed them peanut butter and jelly sandwiches (Jon's favorite) and tomato sandwiches (Bob's favorite).

"There is no doubt in my mind that Jon was to make this trip, and that I should be along to help out," Bob said via email from the road.

Each new day on the road brought new appreciation, new challenges, and new epiphanies for Jon, who didn't suffer one seizure along the way. His sidekick support team, Bob, also discovered a newfound appreciation for America the Benevolent.

"Jon and I were sitting in a restaurant tonight," Bob said

Connect your thoughts

in an email, "talking about all we have seen and the special people we have met along the way. This has brought home to us just how special this country and her people are."

Special, indeed. Throughout Jon and Bob's nine-state trip across the heartland, they repeatedly experienced the goodness, kindness, and generosity of complete strangers. On the third day of Jon's trip, before Bob joined up with him, he got his first flat tire outside a little village called Heyworth, Illinois. He had no spare inner tubes and no idea of the nearest store, and his cell phone was dying. "I was utterly stranded," Jon said.

He called his little brother to surf the Internet for the nearest store, but then his phone died and he didn't get a reply. An hour later, a stranger approached him out of no-where. "Are you Jon?" the man asked. "Yes," Jon replied. The man's name was Mark, a village trustee. "Your brother called the village hall," he told Jon. "We've been looking for you."

Jon was flabbergasted. As luck, fate, or connections would have it, the village trustees were having a meeting that night and Mark was at the hall preparing for it when the call came in. Village officials even had the local sheriff looking for Jon. "I was literally a wanted man," Jon said. Mark drove Jon fifteen miles to a bike shop in Bloomington, where he bought inner tubes and the equipment he needed. He then drove Jon back to Heyworth and hauled Jon and his bike to his house to fix it. He offered Jon a shower. He offered Jon dinner. Jon instead accepted a few homegrown tomatoes from the trustee. "I was truly humbled and moved by their kindness," Jon recalled.

This sort of slice-of-Americana experiences peppered Jon and Bob's entire trek.

Another example took place when they couldn't find a hotel or motel with any vacancies near Greensburg, Kansas, and had to sleep in a Wal-Mart parking lot. "It was a long sleepless night and all that goes along with being scrunched up in a van with a bicycle," Bob said. The next night they found out why there were no hotel vacancies there: In May, a tornado wiped out most of Greensburg and nearly every motel room in that region was still filled with its now-homeless residents.

"I no longer feel emotionally drained and upset from trying to sleep in a van parked in a parking lot," Bob explained after realizing why the local hotels were filled. There also was the time Jon spotted four tiny kittens purring on the side of a road in Arizona, and he just couldn't pass them up. He stopped, put them in his saddle bag, and retraced his path several miles back to a hotel, "meowing" to them along the way. The hotel owner, an animal lover, promised to find a home for the kittens, so Jon kept biking westward to his dream job.

Jon's most cherished memory came when he stopped to visit his Great Aunt Grace on the same farm in Vandalia, Missouri, where his paternal grandmother was raised. While there, Jon called his father so that he could also talk to Aunt Grace. "She was overjoyed," Jon said of her reconnecting with her Hoosier relatives. Two weeks later, while Jon pedaled across another state, Aunt Grace died.

"If it hadn't been for the bike trip, I never would have seen my Aunt Grace again, my dad would never have been able to talk to her that one last time, and I never would have known what it's like to feel like I was home again," Jon said. "It was simply one of the most wonderful moments of my life."

The culmination of such events and people profoundly changed Jon, allowing him to reflect not only on his new friends but also on himself. "Hearing their stories, their dreams and secret pains and regrets, it made me realize how very fortunate I am, and how many people would love to be able to do something like this," he said.

At the 2,002-mile mark, while trekking through scorching hot Arizona, the rear axle on Jon's bike broke from too much wear and tear. Bob had to drive 200 miles round-trip to Phoenix to get it repaired, and to buy a new rear wheel rim, a new chain, and two new tires. A day later, Jon was back on the road. His next destination: California.

Jon's magical mystery bicycle ride ended almost a month after it began, when the California dreamer arrived in Santa Monica and baptized his borrowed bike in the Pacific Ocean, some 2,500 miles from his starting point.

"I'm mentally and physically exhausted and feel like I could sleep for a week, but at the same time I have a hunger for life I haven't felt in a long time," Jon said. "I can't wait to see what each new day will bring."

When we caught up to Jon and Bob a few months later, Bob said he had a renewed attitude, feeling and reverence for life since putting his life on hold to accompany Jon.

"At my age," he said, "attitude, feelings, and reverence for life are important. What more can a man ask for?"

Oh, and what about that high-tech bicycle he let Jon borrow, the one that's back again in Bob's shed, with sand from the Pacific Ocean still on the front tire?

"I keep saying I should clean off the sand but … it brings back many memories," Bob said fondly.

As for Jon, he has first-hand advice for others who want to connect more with themselves: "Never quit. Never give up. Never stop. A negative attitude will only kill your dreams. Keep on pedaling for *your* connections."

Which people in your life make you the happiest or most relaxed? Which people make you feel the most connected without even trying?

It's no secret that many of us — probably *too* many of us — allow our lives to coast along aimlessly without direction, purpose, or a destination.

We're using Jon's story as a reminder that you can't always wait in life's garage or back-alley to find new connections. You need to put forth effort, make a plan, and pedal your own dream, first to yourself, then to others.

More importantly, it's not simply reaching out to others in our stream of possible connections, but also *telling them* what you want or need. Jon and Bob both did this, too. They *told* each other what they needed, and then acted on it.

What do *you* want from the landscape of human connections in your life? Have you ever told them in plain and simple terms? If so, have you reminded them lately? If not, what are you waiting for? These people may be in your life at this time for a reason. (Remember, *everyone* happens for a reason.) Your goal is to seek these connections, every day, by making it part of your daily thinking.

Here are a few more reminders:

•Recharge, refocus, and rethink the existing connections in your life.

•Ask yourself questions. Remember, it's all about the questions, not the answers. If you ask the right questions, the right answers will eventually materialize.

•Repeatedly remind yourself that you don't know as much about your life as you think you do.

If it helps, just think of the fabled Nacirema tribe. The who? Let us explain.

The Nacirema is a very odd clan of people who live

between the Canadian Cree and the Tarahumare of Mexico, migrating from the east, as legend goes. According to Nacirema mythology, their nation was originated by a cultural hero named Notgnihsaw. And its backward people even to this day focus strongly on the human body and its appearance to others in the tribe. The group's fundamental belief is that the human body is ugly, even repulsive, and they use all kinds of primitive rituals and ceremonies to avert the body's natural characteristics. Every household has one or more shrines devoted to this very purpose.

The shrine's focal point is typically a box or chest that is built into a wall, filled with several magical potions, charms and elixirs. And tribesmen who are rich or powerful have

Do you give what you want?
For example, if you want friendship,
do you give it to others?
If you want trust, do you trust others?

multiple shrines in their homes. Beneath these charm chests are small wells where, each morning, family members bow their heads and cleanse themselves in a holy water, which comes from the community's "Water Temple" where priests conduct daily rituals to make the liquid pure again. Here, they perform a daily mouth ritual, involving the insertion of a small bundle of hog hairs or something similar, affixed with certain magical powders mixed into a pasty substance. Here, they bathe and perform private excretory acts in the secrecy of these shrines, by the use of a sacred vessel called a "teliot."

The Nacirema obey several strange customs and beliefs, including the notion that parents bewitch their own children and, later in life, the bewitched then seek a witch doctor called "the listener" to exorcise these evils. Mothers in particular are suspected of putting such a curse on their children while teaching them secret body rituals.

Some of the bewitched, betrayed by their bodies over time, perform ritual fasts to rid themselves of flesh, while others gorge themselves with food to feed the inner demons.

And on and on this legend goes, documenting in familiar detail the odd body rituals and cultural beliefs of the Nacirema tribe.

If you haven't figured it out yet, the Nacirema tribe is us, with American spelled backward — about as backward as our beliefs must seem to more "primitive" cultures. In fact, this eye-opening cultural self-portrait was penned more than a half century ago by the anthropologist Harold Miner.

Miner's essay, "Body Ritual Among the Nacirema," has since been used time and again by college professors as an insightful illustration for their know-it-all students. And now it can be used by you, too, as a reminder about your self awareness. Or the lack thereof.

Our point: Connecting with yourself means first admitting that you may not know everything about your life, your friends, your coworkers, or your family, let alone your future connections. And now is the time to reexamine everyone in your life to see how they may be able to connect you with what you want, what you need, or what you dream about.

Maureen can attest to the power of dreaming about a connection and then making it happen, through sheer per-

Do you like what you see when you look in the mirror? Physically? Emotionally? Psychologically? If not, why not?

sistence, if nothing else.

On Dec. 7, 2001, Maureen's husband underwent heart surgery. His prognosis wasn't too good, and Maureen left the hospital thinking her husband of then 46 years might not make it.

She returned home, sat on the couch, prayed, and fell asleep. During her nap, Maureen dreamed that someone knocked on the couple's door. When she opened it, actor Michael Clarke Duncan greeted her. That's right, Michael Clarke Duncan, the towering actor who starred in "The Green Mile," "Armageddon," and other popular films.

To this day, Maureen doesn't know why she dreamt of Duncan of all people on such a trying night in her life. It was Duncan who entered her home and it was Duncan who asked her to sit on his lap. Then, in her dream, Duncan told Maureen that her husband would survive the risky surgery and everything would be fine.

Maureen recalls resting her head on Duncan's shoulder and falling asleep. The next morning, she returned to the hospital and found out her husband's surgery was indeed a success. And they have since celebrated their 50th wedding anniversary.

But Maureen still felt Duncan did "something" memorable that night, even if he simply calmed her fears. She knew that he didn't actually *do* anything. Still, she wanted him to know. She contacted Jerry to get the word out.

Jerry wrote a column about Maureen, her dream, and her wish to somehow connect with Duncan, her newfound "guardian angel." The day his column ran, Jerry also flew to Hollywood to look for Duncan.

OK. Not really. He *did* fly to Los Angeles that day, but not to look for Duncan. He flew there for a college newspaper convention. However, while there, Jerry got an excited phone call from Maureen.

Guess who called her home at precisely 11:57 a.m. that day? And guess who just happened to *not* be home to receive the call?

"Hello, this is Michael Clarke Duncan," the deep-voiced man said on the couple's answering machine.

Maureen's husband figured it was a prank call. It wasn't. Duncan continued his phone message, saying, "I am trying to get in touch with Maureen … I read the news article and it touched my heart …"

Maureen's husband eventually realized that the voice belonged to Duncan and he quickly picked up the call. He ended up speaking to Duncan for a few minutes, and Duncan even congratulated him on his successful surgery.

"When he calls back," Richard said, "it will make her day, her year, heck, her life."

"There's got to be some kind of connection here," he told Jerry. "I know there's a connection between him and Maureen and my surgery and, well, everyone. But Maureen simply wouldn't give up making this particular connection."

Connect your thoughts

This is another point we're trying to make. Sometimes connections need work, persistence, even relentlessness. Of course, Maureen's dreamy connection to Duncan could be considered comical. However, she *did* make it happen. Didn't she?

So can you, with *your* connections. Don't forget to use the provided "Connect Your Thoughts" margin to write down all your possible connections when they come to mind.

Contrary to Maureen's situation, some connections have a way of finding *you*. It's your job to identify them when they do. Just ask Phil, whose chronic vision problems led him to a second-hand prayer. The next thing he knew, a genuine "miracle" happened.

Initially, Phil almost strolled right past the Church of the Immaculate Conception, but then he heard organ music. It sounded peaceful. It sounded joyous. It sounded like a reason to go inside. He did. He sat on a pew near the altar, not exactly to pray, but to have an informal chat with God. The organ music serenaded the one-way conversation. He talked. God listened.

Phil, a civil engineer by trade, never found it necessary to erect false pretenses to speak with the Lord. He instead spoke from the heart on that January morning in 2001 at the motherhouse of The Sisters of Providence.

"God, you've probably heard about my eye problems," he said. "Of course you have, you're God. Well, anyway …"

Since he was six, Phil suffered through poor eyesight, forcing him to wear thick glasses that looked like the bottom of pop bottles. By the time he was in his fifties, his vision seriously worsened, with advanced cataracts in both eyes, myopia, astigmatism, and blurred hope for corrective surgeries. In 1998, he became director of facilities management at Saint Mary-of-the-Woods. After too many years in the corporate rat race, he sought a workplace that valued humans as more than just resources. He found it. There, he fell in love with the quiet, peaceful 1,200-acre grounds, founded by Blessed Mother Theodore (Anne-Therese) Guerin in 1840. She came from France after a request from the bishop.

Phil remembers looking out his guest house window one morning during the interview process. He saw horses prancing on a fresh blanket of snow, their breaths visible in the crisp air. He saw what Mother Theodore had seen 158

Do you spend your free time doing things to connect with what you truly love to do? Or is it bogged down by bad habits, old dramas, and ball-and-chain obligations?

years earlier. He also saw his future.

"This," he told his wife, "is a joyous place."

On Sept. 21, 2000, Phil underwent surgery on his left eye, the worst of his vision problems. It helped. A second surgery, on his right eye, took place a month later. The procedure didn't help. A specialist was referred and a corneal transplant was recommended. Unfortunately, the procedure carried the risk of potential blindness.

Phil was scared, unsure of the right decision. He sought respite. He sought help. He took some time to consider his future. This is when Phil first heard the welcoming organ music inside the church. He ditched work for ten minutes to have a chat with God.

He asked for help. He asked for peace of mind. He certainly didn't ask for a miracle cure. Before leaving the pew, he also chatted with the essence of Mother Theodore, considering that he was, in a way, her employee and all. Plus, he figured he'd cover all his holy bases while there.

"Blessed Mother, if you have any intercessions with God, I'd really appreciate some help here," he said, respectfully. Figuring he had goofed off from work long enough, he left the church, exhaled a big sigh, and said to himself, "OK, I can do this."

As a kid, Phil regularly attended an American Baptist church, either willingly or dragged by his father, a lay minister. Phil has always been a believer, but nothing over the top or preachy. He didn't necessarily take the job at The

Sisters of Providence for its Roman Catholic fringe benefits, but he certainly wouldn't reject them either.

When he looked in the mirror that day, to see if he needed a shave, he had a hard time explaining what he saw. The chronic droopiness and redness in his right eye were gone. The swelling, too. "That's odd," he told himself. He also told his wife, Debbie, a registered nurse. She asked, "Can you see out of it any better?" "Not completely," he replied. "Then it isn't restored," she said.

Wishful thinking, he figured. He went back to his doctor, the one who had scheduled the cornea transplant.

The doctor looked through some high-tech medical tool into Phil's eye and said, "Hmmm." Phil asked, "Hmmm what?"

"Your eye is better. You don't need surgery."

"I beg your pardon?" Phil asked.

The doctor asked what specialist Phil had visited or what he had done to help his eye.

"I said a prayer," Phil told him.

The doctor told him, "Whatever you did, worked."

A month or so later, after Phil's eyesight went from 20/50 to nearly 20/20, he nonchalantly retold his story to some of the sisters at the convent.

Connect your thoughts

"That's a miracle," they told him.

"Well yeah, I guess it is," he replied, interpreting the word "miracle" in its common usage, not its religious usage. No, they said, that's a "miracle of God."

This is when Phil's life really changed. This is when his miraculously restored eyesight caught the attention of the Roman Catholic Church, the Vatican, and officials with the Cause for the Beatification and Canonization of Mother Theodore.

Long after Mother Theodore's death in 1856, she was unofficially credited with curing the cancer of a fellow sister after prayers were said at her grave site in October, 1908.

The cause to make her a saint — making her only the eighth saint from this country at the time — began in 1909, with a rigorous, complex process of investigative work, interviews, formal trials, and intense scrutiny of her life and teachings.

The oft-ill teacher and nurse came to the United States in 1840 with five sister companions to bring religion and education to a dense, wilderness territory. They opened eleven schools, two orphanages, and an eventual workplace for Phil.

In his book "Making Saints," author Kenneth Woodward writes, "Christianity is unthinkable without sinners and unlivable without saints." A saint is a person who lived a life of heroic Christian virtue and who is believed to be surely in heaven with God. In the Roman Catholic Church, there is a lengthy process for naming saints. Two miracles have to occur. The first after the candidate's death. The second after the candidate's beatification. A miracle is defined as an observable event or effect that cannot be explained by laws of nature, but only as a direct action of God.

It was not until 1997 that Pope John Paul II accepted Mother Theodore's 1908 healing as a miracle, clearing the way for her beatification, and calling her "a perfect blend of humanness and holiness."

And it was not until October, 1998, during a beatification ceremony, that Mother Theodore was given the name Blessed Mother Theodore, ninety years after her first posthumous miracle. All that was needed for her sainthood was a second miracle. And along came Phil and his oh-by-the-way prayer to her holiness.

"If you have God's ear," he told her that fateful day, "I would appreciate it."

Two years later, a formal trial in the Archdiocese of Indianapolis determined that Phil's miracle should be attributed to Mother Theodore's intercession. In 2005, three distinct groups in Rome also approved it as such.

On Feb. 22, 2006, during a ceremony inside the Church of

Connect your thoughts

the Immaculate Conception, Sister Marie Kevin Tighe, vice postulator of Mother Theodore's Cause for Sainthood, admitted that Mother Theodore cannot reverse the laws of nature.

"But we do believe that because she is close to God, she has what is called intercessory power," she said. "When we ask for her help, we are asking her to intercede with God for us and for our needs. When an unusual request is granted, and when there is no natural or medical explanation, it is declared a miracle."

Phil wasn't so sure at first, going through several stages to get a handle on things. First, he openly challenged the concept of belief without proof. "I'm an engineer," Phil said inside the Church of the Immaculate Conception. "This," he said, grabbing a marble column in the church, "is something I can touch, I can see." But a miracle?

He then asked, "Why me?" The sisters replied, "Why not?" Phil questioned the heavens. "What did I do to deserve this?" The miracle was an act of love, a blessing, he was told.

"But I'm not even Catholic," he countered. That doesn't matter, he was told. Mother Theodore never discriminated when it was a matter of whom she might help.

Phil then thought some kind of moral or religious obligation would be expected of him. The sisters insisted that no dogmatic strings were attached. At that point, Phil considered converting to Catholicism.

In early-October, 2006, Phil became the eye of a media hurricane. The BBC shadowed him for a documentary. National newspapers interviewed him. Even foreign press agencies contacted him. On Oct. 15 of that year, Phil visited Rome to take part in the long-awaited canonization of

Mother Theodore inside the Vatican. He and his wife of forty two years were in attendance when Pope Benedict XVI conducted the ceremony.

Before flying to Rome, Phil didn't quite grasp his exalted place in history. He envisioned himself as simply an ordinary guy in an extraordinary situation. "Like that Grateful Dead song, what a long, strange trip it's been," he said outside the church.

After all Phil has been through, he still seems more practical than metaphysical. The first thing he did after his vision was restored by God was to buy a pair of sunglasses. He also discovered some truths about himself, his faith, and his personal connections.

"For me, it was all about the connections I made since

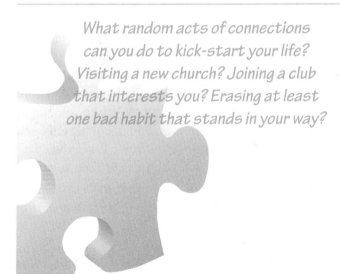

What random acts of connections can you do to kick-start your life? Visiting a new church? Joining a club that interests you? Erasing at least one bad habit that stands in your way?

the day I offered that particular prayer."

And those very-human connections, he says, have been quite, well, miraculous.

Our point isn't that *your* connections will have similarly miraculous results. It's more to show that people such as Phil *make* their connections happen. Let's face it, if a Baptist civil engineer can stroll into a Catholic church to have a brief chat with God, with absolutely zero expectations, then you should be able to identify — and approach — absolutely anyone in your daily orbit as a possible *connection*. Stranger things have happened. Just ask Phil.

Think about it: Can the guy at your dry cleaners be a helpful connection for you? How about that female co-worker to whom you rarely talk? The bowling team member who keeps to himself? Or…? You get the idea.

Do you see how many potential connections there are in your life? Somehow they may have become invisible to you. That's what this chapter is all about: Removing the social blinders we all wear. First look inward before looking outward. In short, better to connect with yourself before connecting with others. If you get stuck, try to remember how people like Jon, Maureen, and Phil connected with themselves while connecting with others. Like you, they are simply ordinary people who connected themselves to extraordinary circumstances of varying degrees.

Dennis feels most connected to himself through songs and movies that seem to resonate with certain situations at various times in his life. For example, he remembers back in college one late night cramming for a final exam at the end of a tough semester.

The next day, after he took the test, he didn't feel good about its outcome and was really down on himself. On the way back to his apartment, he remembered a new movie just released, titled "What About Bob," with Bill Murray. Murray plays a hapless but not hopeless patient named Bob Wiley who follows his highly respected psychiatrist on his family vacation. There he practices "baby steps" to better mental health while winning over the doctor's family, but also driving the doctor crazy.

Dennis and his roommate watched the movie that night and laughed out loud the entire time. To this day, Dennis still isn't sure if his laughter erupted from the movie's plot and script, Murray's comedic chops, or simply because he needed an emotional release at that exact time in his life. Regardless, it immediately changed his mood and spirits. Fifteen years later, he still remembers its lesson.

These days, Dennis is so far gone with his passion for movies that he has trouble watching them without finding *some* connection to help ground him. He always seems to find a way to connect the film's story, plot, or characters to

Connect your thoughts

his own life. If he feels in a rut, or somehow disconnected with himself, the first thing he usually does is rent a movie or visit a theatre.

Since then, he's noticed how certain movies — and songs, books, and places, for that matter — have a way of tapping into certain emotions in his psyche, as well as certain key points in his life. This same phenomenon holds true for all of us, and it's why songs, movies, and certain places affect different listeners or viewers in completely different ways. They allow us to interpret them through the prism of our own understanding and experiences.

Have you ever heard a song from your youth and immediately flashed back to that age, the euphoria, sadness, or wonderment? Have you ever visited a certain place that continues to spark the same emotions? Remember, a "place" is a space that has memories, such as, say, your grandmother's kitchen and cooking, or the site of your first kiss. Think for a moment, do you visit spaces or places?

Or have you ever watched a movie for the second (or tenth) time because it always has a way of reconnecting you with you? One film in particular has become requisite viewing for cousins Dennis and Jerry when they're feeling a bit disconnected from things and from themselves. It's called *ironically* "Cousins," a 1989 remake of the popular French romantic comedy titled "Cousin, Cousine."

The film stars Ted Danson and Isabella Rossellini, two endearing people whose not-so-endearing spouses are having an affair. Danson and Rossellini's characters meet at a family wedding after their spouses steal away into the wilds of infidelity. They later meet on their own, find consolation together about their cheating mates, and eventually fall in love, literally sailing into the sunset. It's a charming, humorous and, at times, poignant movie with intoxicating characters, infectious dialogue, and memorable scenes. One character, Vince, steals the show as Danson's cantankerous yet lovable father. His lines are both timely and timeless.

In one scene, at a cemetery, the lonely widower declined to join a funeral group, quipping to his grandson, "At my age, you don't want to get too close to an open grave."

The grandson then asked why Vince didn't come into the church, either. Vince replied, "God makes me nervous when you get him indoors. Besides, I don't like to see people in their coffins. They always look so much smaller without their spirits."

Later, while trying to flirt with an older woman, Vince said, "I like your shoes. They show off your bubble-gum toes." And after she reluctantly accepted his dinner invitation, he replied, "You've made an old man very happy!"

"You're not so old," the woman said.

"Yeah, I know," he replied, "and I'm not so happy."

Connect your thoughts

After he returned from his "hot date" that night, his grandson asked how it went.

"Can you keep a secret?" Vince asked, leaning in close.

"Yeah," his grandson replied, also leaning in close.

"So can I," Vince said, smirking.

Vince also gave his son, Larry, played by Danson, food for thought when it came to truly connecting with himself: "You've got only one life to live. You can either make it chicken shit or chicken salad."

Larry eventually made chicken salad by finally asking Rossellini's character, Maria, "How about spending the rest of your life with me?"

"Larry, I would love to," Maria replied.

In the end, they ride off into the proverbial sunset on Larry's refurbished boat.

After watching this movie, Dennis and Jerry always feel more attached to their faith, hopes, and dreams. (*For a list of our favorite "connections" movies, visit our Web site, www.connectionsbook.com.*)

Maybe the best way for you to reconnect is by doing something completely different, such as visiting a park, or skydiving, or quietly taking in nature, or going for a run, or calling your mother, or pouring your thoughts into a journal. Whatever it is, this is the time — right now — to figure it out. Go ahead, relax, breathe, take a moment, and use the margins in this book to write down your personal "connections to yourself."

We want to share with you a famous line from American author and satirist Samuel Clemens, aka Mark Twain. The famous wordsmith took his maritime pen name from how riverboats measured a shallow water's depth, as in, "Mark twain!'" which literally means by the mark of two fathoms.

Twain once said the difference between using the right word and the almost right word is the difference between lightning and a lightning bug. The same goes with human connections in your lives. Some people will connect with you immediately like a strike of lightning. Others will flutter about like mere lightning bugs. And that's to be expected. Not every new connection you make will stay afloat. Some may sink. But you have to at least try to connect, develop a relationship, explain to them what you want, need, or aspire to be. See if the ship sails. Otherwise, your life will remain dry-docked in regrets and landlocked from not connecting with yourself.

What movies do you resonate with? Why do you think you connect to them? How about your favorite songs? Favorite places?

Connecting with Yourself
ACTION ITEMS

The following action steps can help spark your brainstorming process.

1. Find the meaning in your life's connections by keeping in mind, "Everyone happens for a reason." Look back and list the five most powerful influences that shaped your life and write down why. These can be positive or negative influences.

2. Read more. Instead of simply using your own personal references, utilize connections of others through books to improve your life and expand your horizons.

3. Be yourself. People will connect and resonate with the real you. Ask those close to you for honest feedback about yourself. Be strong. It may sting.

4. Write a journal of all of the potential connections you came across each day in a social or professional setting. You'll be surprised to how many connections you are exposed.

5. Connect with your family origin. Understanding your past and your parents might help you connect with who you really are.

6. Try random acts of making connections. Go to a movie. Try attending a different church. Do things you wouldn't normally do. You never know where or when you can make a connection that will change your life or the lives of others.

7. Write down three people's lives you would want to connect with or influence.

Connect your thoughts

Connection (ke nek'shen), noun —
"associates or friends considered
as having influence or power"

Connecting In the Workplace

Dr. Mehmet Oz, the familiar-faced medical expert who always wears his trademark blue surgical scrubs on "The Oprah Winfrey Show," didn't hesitate when we asked him for his first career connection.

"My key connection took place at seven-years old," Dr. Oz says matter-of-factly, as if he'd been waiting for someone to ask him this very question. Dr. Oz, who's often called "America's doctor" by media and fans, grew up in Wilmington, Delaware, the son of two Turkish immigrants.

As a boy, young Mehmet once stood inside Patterson's Ice Cream shop in his hometown, next to his father. The question arose, what would young Mehmet be when he grew up? He said he didn't know. His father, a cardiac surgeon, told him in no uncertain terms he should always have a plan, a goal, a destination, even if he changes his mind later.

With that advice, the youngster didn't hesitate: "OK," he told his father, "I want to be a heart surgeon." The rest, as they say, is his-story. He attended Harvard University, became a professor of cardiac surgery at Columbia University, and later became the friendly but firm face for better health and wellness to millions of readers and television-land patients.

When we asked Dr. Oz why he chose that specific profession, besides following in his father's footsteps, he replied, "It sounded like a pretty cool career. And it is." He went on to become an award-winning, best-selling author and also the middle-aged poster child for healthful living. He has since accumulated innumerable honors while writing countless medical abstracts, publications, and thesis papers.

In the November, 2007, issue of Spirituality and Health Magazine, Dr. Oz noted something the authors of this book have known for years: everyone has a purpose in this world. This realization only echoes this book's mantra, he says.

"Yes, I've learned that everyone really does happen for a reason," he says. "My life has illustrated this time and again."

Dr. Oz also co-authored the 2007 book exploring the cellular-based aspects of aging, titled, "YOU: Staying Young: The Owner's Manual for Extending Your Warranty." He is convinced that the human body is genetically designed to live between 100 and 120 years.

Remember, the average life expectancy of an American increased from 47 years to 77 years during the 20th century, and that figure is expected to be extended even more during this century. With this in mind, let us remind you it's never too late to find new career connections in your workplace, or to reconnect with old ones. This holds true whether you're 37, 67, or — if you believe in the medical wizardry of Dr. Oz — even 97 years old. "We simply need to change our perception of aging," he told us with his familiar chuckle.

This is exactly the same outlook we need to take regarding how human connections affect our job, our workplace, and our careers. We simply need to change our perceptions. Not as a business tool to climb the professional ladder. That's called networking. Although there certainly is value in networking, there are hundreds of books already on the market on how to get a promotion, change careers mid-life, or become a billionaire by age forty.

We're talking about viewing your job as a re-energized conduit for sparking new connections, pure and simple. Where else do you get a daily opportunity to meet so many

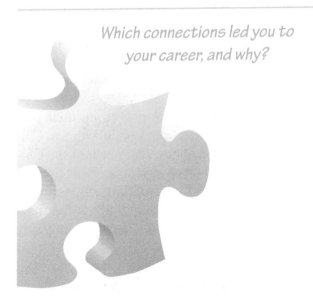

Which connections led you to your career, and why?

different people, fresh faces, or the general public while getting paid to do so?

Remember Walt and Marlene, the older couple who collected decades of "401(k) of the soul" memories, and who first introduced the notion of marking life with an imaginary tape measure? They too had a similar career connection to share, and it immediately came to Walt's mind when he heard about this chapter.

As we told you earlier in these pages, Walt was a working man's man who quit high school to work at dredging waterways, from the St. Lawrence Seaway in upper New York to across the entire Great Lakes basin. For fourteen years, he earned an honest day's dollar at various waterways which needed clearing or deepening. Out of geographical pride or just plain stubbornness, Walt always kept a New York license plate on his car.

To this day, when you ask Walt where he calls "home," it's not where he's lived the past half-century, in the Midwest. It's where he began making memories with Marlene, in Upper New York.

In June, 1964, he and Marlene packed up their new Pontiac Bonneville and traveled from Lorain, Ohio, to Chicago for Walt to help dredge the south branch of the Chicago River. Another job, another paycheck, Walt figured. When winter hit, he was laid off from his job, as usual, so he found work at the American Ship Yard on the city's south side. That job soon froze up, too, in the frigid Windy City.

In February, 1965, Walt wasn't sure what to do next. Then it happened. An incident that changed his life. A chance encounter Walt remembers even four decades later as if it were yesterday morning. His unforgettable career connection.

One cold night, he and Marlene visited a coin-operated Laundromat just across the state line. In those days, not everyone owned a washer and dryer, especially young families on the move. Inside the Laundromat, another couple kept peeking at them near the dryers. Walt and Marlene couldn't figure out why. Finally, the husband wandered over and came out with it.

"So," the stranger asked, "are you folks from New York?"

"Yes, we are," replied Walt, "we're from Oswego."

"Oswego?" the man asked. "My wife lives close to there,

Does your career seem too much like work?
What is holding you back from finding a
more rewarding job or career?

in Old Forge, just north of Utica."

Then Walt had a question of his own for the man.

"How'd you know we're from New York?"

"Your license plate," the man replied. "I saw it and I had to ask."

The two couples got to talking and at some point the stranger, whose name was Ed, asked Walt what he did for a living.

"Dredging," Walt said, before noting he just got laid off.

"Would you be interested in pile-driving?" Ed asked.

Not once in Walt's life did he ever spend a day at pile-driving, surprising for a man whose hands could swallow handshakes whole and whose body was built like a human pile-driver. Walt didn't hesitate to answer.

"Hell yeah," Walt said.

Ed, an engineer for American Bridge, gave Walt the name and phone number of the company's hiring agent. Walt began pile-driving for American Bridge and other companies, never looking back in his life's rearview mirror. In June, 1996, more than thirty-two years after meeting Ed, Walt retired. To this day, he's still collecting a pension from that work, all thanks to Ed. And, don't forget, his beat-up New York license plate.

Once, on a trip back home to upper New York, Walt and Marlene made a special trip to visit Ed and his wife, Tina. Walt had something to say to Ed, something on his mind for four decades.

"I told him I had a beautiful life because of that night at the Laundromat. It was a turning point for me, a profound *connection*," Walt says. "I just wanted him to know that."

Walt didn't realize he had a pivotal connection in his life until he remembered that special night. It all came rushing back. It all came together. That's when Walt learned that not only does everything happen for a reason. Also, *everyone* happens for a reason. In Walt's case, it was Ed.

Who's your workplace connection? Or have you not found that person yet? Whether it happened decades ago, as with Ed, or possibly occurs tomorrow at your workplace, it's all about a new awareness of connections.

Jerry put this new awareness into practice one day at his newspaper columnist job. He received a call that day from a health magazine editor who had a quick question for him. The editor, whom Jerry didn't know, simply wanted to know the correct spelling of a woman's name from a story Jerry had written months earlier. This call could have been just another phone chat on just another busy day with just another editor — nothing more. Instead, it changed Jerry's life. All because of *Connections* (the book, with a capital C).

Connect your thoughts

The newspaper story Jerry wrote was about a local woman who was diagnosed with Non-Hodgkin's Lymphoma, a deadly cancer, and how she defeated it by doing her homework. Too many patients diagnosed with deadly diseases were dying because they weren't taking personal responsibility for their own health, she believed. In her case, she made dozens of phone calls, clicked through hundreds of Internet sites, and traveled to distant conferences to find the best treatment for her deteriorating condition. She also studied cutting-edge therapies and upcoming clinical trials, eventually taking part in a free clinical trial at the famed Mayo Clinic in Rochester, Minnesota. There, she began her recovery; and, by the time Jerry met with her, the cancer had already been in remission for five years.

This was just another typical daily newspaper story for Jerry — nothing more, nothing less. The woman's name was Mary Colclasure. The magazine editor chose her story to run in an upcoming edition of a national health publication — a publication Jerry didn't even know existed. One problem for the magazine editor, though, was she needed the correct spelling of the patient's name. The editor asked if it was "Coclasure" or "Colclasure"? Jerry admitted that Colclasure's name can be somewhat confusing to spell. He quickly provided the correct spelling.

Again, another typical question about another story by another editor. But — and this is a big "but" — before the editor could hang up the phone, Jerry tried making a new connection in his career. The entire exchange lasted only two minutes. However, it's still paying dividends today, thanks to Connections.

"Can I ask you a quick question?" Jerry asked the magazine editor.

"Sure," she replied.

"Can you tell me more about your magazine?" he asked.

The editor politely obliged, filling him in on its editorial content, its distribution areas, and its choice of freelance contributors.

Jerry quickly asked another question.

"Do you need any new writers?" he asked.

"No, not at this time," the editor replied. But she told him to send in his résumé and story clips if he wanted, "in case something comes up."

The editor hung up. Jerry hung up. That was that, right? Wrong. After the editor's obligatory gesture, Jerry followed through. He sent in his résumé and clips and, a month later, she called him back. "Are you still interested in writing for us?" she asked him. "I think we have a story for you."

Jerry couldn't believe his "luck." For years, he had tried to launch a freelance writing career, but to no avail. He sent story and column queries to countless magazines and other publications. Locally. Regionally. Nationally. He received rejection after rejection. Nothing was different between his

Connect your thoughts

writing years earlier and his writing on that day in 2004. His résumé was pretty much the same. His writing clips were pretty much the same. He turned nothing into something that day. He turned a stranger in his workplace into a new career connection.

The health-related story he was asked to write led to another, then another. The editor later shared Jerry's work with a different editor, who offered him a story for a different publication, directed at senior citizens. One story led to another, and he received another assignment from a separate publication, aimed at wellness education. Since that very first phone call — completely out of the blue and totally unexpected — Jerry has written hundreds of freelance stories for various publications, enabling him to supplement his columnist income. Most importantly, this enabled him to begin this book project. Not only could he write about connections in an abstract way, he could now write about connections in a personal, practical, and hands-on way.

Our point? Jerry changed his perception on how to make a new career connection; and, when the opportunity knocked on his door (or, in this case, called on his phone), he took advantage of it. Was it a stroke of luck that prompted the magazine editor to call him? You bet. But it was Jerry's newfound awareness to making new connections that turned a little luck into a stroke of good fortune.

This is exactly what we're talking about; taking advantage of every opportunity which comes our way, *and* being aware enough to do so. Surely such everyday opportunities come into your workplace, too. Begin looking for them. If you stay anchored to your same-old perceptions, these opportunities will sink any chances you have for new connections.

After work has ended, you can also explore your life's "third place" for finding business-oriented alliances with others. Sociologist Ray Oldenburg best describes the concept of a "third place" in his book *The Great, Good Place*.

Most of us have two primary places — home and work. But there is often a third place where we feel comfortable, anchored, and part of an accepted community of familiar-faced people. Maybe it's a local restaurant, a neighbor-

What is the most important personal connection you have in your workplace, and why?

hood church, or the corner pub, as in the famed TV series "Cheers." Do you remember "Nooooorrrrmmm!" being greeted every day by friendly bar patrons?

In the 21st century, maybe it's one of several social-network sites such as MySpace, Facebook, or LinkedIn, connecting people together in cyberspace. We see millions of users frequenting these cyber-relationship sites, whether they're teenagers seeking "friends," middle-aged baby boomers looking to reconnect with their youth, or senior citizens searching for like-minded users. The goal is the same as it was in the 20th century, or the 15th century, for that matter — to bond with others on a regular basis.

Regardless of time, space, or location, such third places are everywhere in our society, and everyone needs at least one, Oldenburg claims.

We agree. Dennis even found his career connection at a third place location, a local gym, while he waited to play a pick-up basketball game. Dennis waited alongside another player for their game to begin, and struck up a conversation.

The brief sideline chat involved the typical guy-to-guy chatter: Name, occupation, and family information. Dennis, who once owned his own engineering consulting business, discovered the other player was a fellow engineer. "An engineer?" Dennis thought to himself. He immediately began exploring the notion of how to make the most of this possible "career connection." It turned out the other player was a partner at a local engineering firm. Through the course of their pre-game conversation, Dennis learned that the man's firm was looking to expand in an area in which he had a particular strength. One thing led to another and they began a partnership, eventually growing into one of the largest firms in Las Vegas.

Dennis wasn't too surprised. His strongest connections in life are typically related to sports, from relationships with his family, with his closest friends, and even with the love of his life. Dennis met his wife, Heather, while flying on an airplane from Salt Lake City to Las Vegas after playing in a tennis tournament.

Dennis, a frequent flier for business purposes, has learned his favorite time to ponder his connections is when he's on airplanes, another possible "third place" location for him. There, in the Friendly Skies, he's left alone with his thoughts. There, he's able to soar above the cloudiness of the day's stress, problems or worries. There, he has nothing to do but "stare at the stars and dream," before taking action on his thoughts.

That's the key: Taking action, being assertive, and telling others what you're looking for in a job, or a career, just as Dennis did while waiting to shoot some hoop. Otherwise, as the late, great George Carlin once quipped, it's like talking about the weather each day and thinking you'll

Connect your thoughts

someday have an effect on it.

Carlin, by the way, experienced the life-changing epiphany of a missed connection early in his career. It happened before he learned to connect with himself and his iconic gifts as a stand-up comedian. Before his death from heart failure in the summer of 2008, the 71-year-old sharp-witted wordsmith and sharp-tongued social critic told the Associated Press that as a young comic he performed superficial jokes for conservative crowds.

And wrongly so. After a decade of entertaining people who didn't really connect with his preferred style of humor and social commentary, Carlin said, "It finally dawned on me that I was in the wrong place doing the wrong things for the wrong people."

Who do you know to help you advance your career or find a more rewarding job? Coworkers or church contacts? Social groups or family members? Make a list.

Connecting in the Workplace
ACTION ITEMS

The following action steps may help spark your brainstorming process.

1. Seek out people or mentors who have achieved the things you desire in your career, and interview them. Mentors typically want to help and pass on what they've learned. Someone probably connected with and helped them, too.

2. Write down five new connections needed to achieve the next goal in your career. For example:

> •Time-management coaches to reduce/eliminate interruptions, emails, etc.
> •Join a Toastmasters club to become more confident in public speaking
> •Reach out to your colleagues
> •"Connections" coaching! (Visit our Web site for more info)

3. Look to connect with and help others. Law of benefactors: If I succeed, who else does?

4. Attend network events and create dialogues with people.

5. Build trust with your coworkers. People don't trust leaders with whom they don't connect.

*"We're social animals.
We need to have connections."*

*— Dr. Myrna Sarowitz,
clinical psychologist*

Connecting With Others

Gil walked with a bum hip, an old fishing pole, and a wrinkled grocery bag to the Lake Michigan shoreline. Threatening skies and angry lightning arced above the pier, warning him to stay away. The determined eighty-year-old man didn't listen. He reached the water's edge, plunged his hand into the paper bag, and unveiled his preferred form of communication — a homemade, customized-to-scale sailboat, complete with working sails and a waterproof message.

Forget cell phones, e-mail, text messaging, or the iPhone — such high-tech gadgetry is for 21st-century simpletons, Gil figured. He instead chose a centuries-old maritime means of connecting with people. And it still works. On this July evening, Gil gently tossed his little sailboat into the choppy waters and hoped his last-minute adjustment to the red-and-white sails would work in such a stiff, stormy wind.

"If she catches wind, she'll go," he says, never taking his eye off his sea-worthy creation. "I made her to sail. She'll survive the storm."

After months of trial-and-error practice followed by watching recent weather reports for this day, Gil's adjustments worked perfectly. His improvised sailboat caught wind and, within seconds, sailed into the unknown. He didn't even need to use his extended fishing pole to push her into deeper water.

She departed willingly. Gil stood there at the lakeshore and smiled to himself as his sailboat bobbed over the rough waves and disappeared into the lake. "Well, we'll see," he says. What he meant was, we'll see if someone finds the boat, its message, and its timeless hope — that two total strangers can still find each other, and connect, through some sort of cosmic randomness or grand design fate. Don't laugh. It's already happened several times for Gil.

Since childhood, Gil always enjoyed making models from scratch. Model airplanes, boats, soapbox racers, automobiles, you name it. For the past twenty-five years, he has made little sailboats as gifts for his grandchildren, a sort of rite of passage. He uses makeshift materials and remnant items from around his home and garage — old fishing line, balsa wood, Styrofoam, leftover modeler's paint, and lead weights for the keel to keep them afloat. "Stuff I had laying around," he explains.

Then, one day back in early 2007, Gil told his wife, Rosemary, "Maybe I'll throw a few in the lake and see what happens." So he did. He equipped seven of them, including a couple made more than twenty years ago, with little waterproof capsules, such as what 35-mm camera film is kept in, and fastened them with fishing line.

Inside each capsule were the same items: a $2 bill for

good luck, a self-addressed stamped envelope, and a tiny note: "Please let me know where and when found. Boat made this winter (for something to do). I would be happy if it would go to a grateful person. Thanks. G.V. Hancock. I'm eighty-years old."

Then he went to two local piers, one in Chicago, and "launched" them, just as he did this past evening. The water current has to be just right, the wind direction just so, and a little lady luck always helps, he said. "It's old-time communication, wherever the four winds take them," he says.

He wasn't sure if any would be found, let alone if the newfound owners would even reply. Maybe all the sailboats would crash onto empty beaches or forever sail unnoticed, he feared. And understandably so. A quarter-century ago, he tossed some message-in-a-bottle missives into the lake hoping for a reply. None ever came.

But his luck to connect with others changed when he launched his new sailboats, which he meticulously numbered in a so-called ship's log. A few weeks later, he received four letters in the mail, from four different people, from four different corners of Lake Michigan. Gil couldn't believe it. Nor could Rosemary.

Connect your thoughts

"Dear sir, it is my pleasure to inform you that #6 made its way to Grand Haven, Michigan. I found it three miles west," wrote Jeffrey, a licensed yacht captain from Chicago.

Jeffrey says he noticed the boat's red sail bobbing in the waves more than 150 miles from where Gil launched it. It stood out like a castaway at sea, he said.

Jeffrey immediately wrote to Gil, gushing, "I was having a bad day and finding #6 made me laugh and feel better the rest of the day and days to follow. It would be my honor to keep #6 and display it at my home."

Jeffrey even took a photo of it outside the U.S. Coast Guard Station in Grand Haven, Michigan, and mailed it to Gil for proof, along with the $2 bill.

Another letter came from Ralph, a 32-year-old man who found boat #5 near his home. Ralph also wrote back to Gil, saying, "The night I found the boat was my first date with my new love. When she saw the note she said it was lucky. One day I will send the boat back out … in hopes to meet someone new."

Boat No. 7 was found by an eighty-year-old man who wrote, "Your sailboat has been retrieved. The $2 bill will go in my wallet as a good luck piece."

Yet another sailboat was found by a young girl named Sydney, who wrote Gil, saying, "I think it was really cool what you did. I always wanted to sail. Thank you!"

One sailboat recipient even put a fresh spin on things by adding two more dollars into the boat and re-launching it. After people heard about Gil's sailboats-to-connect philosophy, he received a ton of letters, congratulating him.

One letter came from Kelly, a woman who enjoys boating with her boyfriend, Chuck. "Your story had me crying and laughing at the same time," she told Gil.

Kelly owns a 53-foot Carver Voyager vessel and, she wrote to Gil, "We would be honored to take you and your family for a ride anytime. P.S. I'm not crazy, I promise!"

Gil couldn't believe that not only were his tiny sailboats found in the massive Great Lake, but his attempts to connect with strangers actually worked. Five of his seven launched sailboats were found, and each new owner replied, as grateful as Gil could have hoped.

To Gil, it's simply about a basic human necessity, a primal need that still pumps through our veins in the 21st century. To connect with other people. He simply took an an-

Which relationships do you wish you had?

cient route with a tried and true method — his homemade sailboats. "It's almost magical," he says with a child's enthusiasm.

Sure, it may *seem* magical, but it's not. You see, Gil acted on his impulse to connect with others. And his idea sailed into the hands — and hearts — of many other people.

Connecting with others can often take place when you *think* you least need them in your busy life — regardless of your age. It doesn't matter which generational group you belong to — the Great Depression Babies, Baby Boomers, Echo Baby Boomers, Generation Y, the YouTube Youthquake, the Millennials, or the Facebook Frat. Everyone has a primal, personal, and permanent longing to connect with others.

Almost everyone also has a similar longing to connect with God or a higher power. Yet when it comes to religion or spirituality, we seem to be losing the ability to connect with our soul as much as we are with others. Let's face it. Hundreds of years ago we knew less about our body and more about our soul. Today, it seems the opposite.

Maybe this explains why nearly one-third of American adults have left the faith in which they were raised, switching either to another religion or to no religion at all. This according to a 2008 report by the Pew Forum on Religion and Public Life. Those of us who claim no ties to any organized religion — the so-called "unaffiliated" — now represent the fourth-largest category of religious identification in this country, the report states.

Other similar studies have shown that half of all believers will jump ship from one religious group to another in their lifetime. Their reasons are as varied as the thousands of denominations in this country. In other words, developing our connections with others — like developing our faith — is an evolutionary process.

Too many of us remain unaffiliated in life, some stranded on distant islands in our youth, others swimming alone in an undertow of uncertainty in our older years. This certainly isn't what happened with John and Jeanette, who shared the same island of happiness and contentment for forty years. They knew from early on in their relationship how to connect with each other. They called it true love.

In November, 1960, John had just received a full scholarship to play basketball for Idaho State University. The tall, lanky twenty-year-old mannish-boy was so excited he carried the scholarship letter wherever he went, including to a dentist appointment.

There he showed the letter to a tall, attractive nineteen-year-old dental assistant, Jeanette.

"Congratulations," she told him politely.

"Thanks," he replied proudly.

Connect your thoughts

And that was that. John soon left for ISU, and Jeanette soon left for Tennessee State University. They both wanted to be teachers.

Fast forward three years. Both John and Jeanette returned home for summer break from college. John just happened to be hanging out with friends across the street from that dental office when he saw Jeanette walking out.

That's when lightning struck. When fate collided with luck. When John said to himself, "Wow, look at her. Someday, she's gonna be mine." And he was right. She did become his.

John and Jeanette began courting that summer. They talked. They laughed. They dreamed. In the fall they returned to their schools, thousands of miles apart.

They wrote letters to each other. They called each other. They soon realized their relationship was special, very special. The months peeled away.

In the summer of 1964 they spent as much time together as possible before returning to school again. For Christmas that year, Jeanette gave John a hand-crafted paddle, symbolizing his fraternity chapter at ISU, which he struggled to co-found. The paddle is adorned with a large "J" merging both their names, with the inscription, "To John... The Love of My Life, Jeanette."

Her gift sealed the deal for John. He was hers for life. He knew it right then and there. She did, too. Of course, they had to return to school again. On Jan. 6, 1965, Jeanette wrote John at ISU, saying, "John, you mean so much to me. I never knew that I could love, care for, want, or need anyone as much as I do you. You are my life. P.S. I promise

I will never run out of time to write you even if I have to write on the back of a stamp and send it as is."

John also returned his love and devotion through an endless roll of stamps.

On June 4, 1965, the day before he graduated college, John walked into a local jeweler and bought Jeanette a wedding ring. Three months later, he proposed. She accepted. He asked her parents for their blessing, and they gave it. A date was set — April 16, 1966, and on that day their two lives melted into one.

"Our love transcended everything else," John recalls. "Everything fell into place."

The young couple worked hard, taught thousands of students, and vacationed often, taking cruises, flights, and car trips together to explore the world. They never had children. Their offspring was their love.

"We had a ball together," John says. "We weren't perfect, but we felt we were special."

And they were. They didn't walk in each other's shadow. They didn't disrespect each other. And they didn't forget the big picture in life, their love affair.

The two educators in love and life eventually earned their master's degrees and became principals at various schools.

Connect your thoughts

They began planning their retirement together, culminating with a trip to Hawaii to celebrate the dawn of their golden years. Fate tarnished their plans.

In 2002, Jeanette was diagnosed with cancer. The couple was devastated, but John made his intentions clear: "I will never abandon you." And he didn't. Prayers, surgery and chemotherapy only delayed the inevitable. Jeanette was forced to retire early. John refused to leave her alone for a minute, so he retired early, too, to become her caregiver.

At John's retirement party, he wrapped his arm around Jeanette and told coworkers, "I'm retiring for her, and she's so worth it."

He fed her. He bathed her. He catered to her. "I wanted her to have the best of care," John says. "I wanted to spend every moment with her." And he did, up until 7:30 p.m. on March 22, 2006, when Jeanette died in the hospital. John held her hand as she drew her last breath. "She put up a good fight but the lord had another plan," John says.

Just after Jeanette's death, John found a handwritten letter she wrote to him in 1965. It's been baffling him ever since with its prophetic wording and vision. Jeanette penned it at age 23, but it reads as if she wrote it at age 63. In it, she strangely looked ahead — and then to the past — as if the young couple had already shared their 40-year marriage and once-in-a-lifetime love affair. Here is an excerpt from that letter.

"Dear John, it is this lonely Saturday afternoon that I feel an overwhelming desire to pledge my love for you. I feel so completely yours, more united than ever before. When I close my eyes I can see a Utopia... in this view you

are expressed in complete physical form ... knowing you assures me of ultimate happiness ... you have shown me many pleasures and happy times.

"It seems that you are every dream I ever dreamed come true. And most assuredly darling, for me there'll never be another you.

"I am feverishly aware of your capabilities and of your ability to guide and comfort me. I am alone now and in my solitude I can almost feel you near me. The powerful impact of your arms around me, and the blessing of your love protecting me.

"Without you, life would have been merely an existence. With you, it was wonderful, everything I have ever hoped for. Thank you very much for your patience and gentleness with me. I shall be eternally grateful. Your fiancée, Jan, July 2, 1965"

John, who at age 69 still has the smile of a tall, lanky mannish-boy, believes Jeanette's letter can serve as her final lesson plan for all of us. It's to put your whole heart into connecting with others, especially if it's a romantic relationship or marriage. Otherwise, you'll languish with regrets or missed connections.

"The only regret I have is losing her," John says. "We

connected from our first smile."

(*To view a photo of John and Jeanette, visit our Web site at www.connectionsbook.com.*)

Connecting with others can be tricky business when it comes to love, romance, and relationships. Let's face it. A good love gone bad is easier to find than a bar date at closing time. Just look at all the messy divorces filed by once seemingly happy "till death do us part" married couples, some coming faster than freezer burn on their wedding cake.

It's certainly not uncommon for a mushy "I love you" to transform into a venomous "I hate you" in a few months, years, or decades later in any relationship. But is love the opposite of hate? We don't think so. Love and hate may seem like polar opposites; but, at the end of the night, they actually share the same bed, blanketed by all the emotional trappings of the day.

The opposite of love is apathy. The two beds in this case are lifetimes apart, separated by a total lack of interest. These sorts of ex-relationships exist totally devoid of emotion. Isn't that what hate is all about anyway — emotion?

Think of it. Have you ever truly hated someone? It takes energy. It takes feelings. In a strange way, it takes passion. It also takes control of your life, and consumes your daily thoughts, doesn't it? Maybe that explains why love, or what people hoped was once "love," easily transforms itself into a deceptive masquerade.

Apathy or indifference, on the other hand, simply moves on, unattached to harsh words, idle threats and heartfelt arguments. This is why apathy or indifference has broken more hearts, dissolved more marriages, and sabotaged more relationships than hate. And this is maybe why Renee was at first reluctant to connect intimately with someone else — until, that is, she met Grant.

Renee connected with Grant during a time in her life when she felt quite happy and content living alone. After losing her first husband in 1977, the Chicago area widow became comfortable as a single, middle-aged woman. Plus, she had become closer to her brother, her friends, and her new lifestyle.

But her daughter worried about her being alone at age

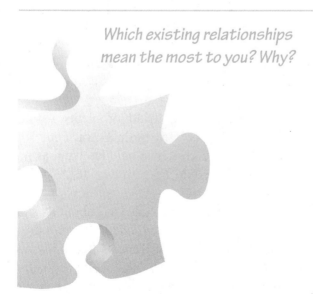

Which existing relationships mean the most to you? Why?

fifty-eight and suggested she put a personal ad in the local newspaper, if for nothing other than companionship. "It sounded like fun to me, so I did," Renee says. She received several replies to her personal ad, including one from a seventy-five-year-old deep-voiced charmer named Grant.

Renee called Grant, and the two young-at-heart romantics immediately hit it off, chatting for hours that night. If women do indeed say 7,000 words a day, on average, and men manage about 2,000, as studies show, that night Renee and Grant surely made up for the previous few weeks without each other's company and conversation.

They later met in person at a local restaurant. They spoke at length, and she became smitten with the tall, handsome widower who lost his wife after forty-seven years of marriage. That night, in the quiet of her empty home, Renee wrote on Grant's personal-ad envelope, "This is the one." He was indeed. The couple married in 1988 and lived happily ever after. "We had a wonderful life together," Renee recalls. (*To view photos of Renee and Grant, visit our Web site at www.connectionsbook.com.*)

In 2005, Grant suffered serious health problems, yet he was still able to celebrate his 93rd birthday, on Feb. 10, 2006. Eight days later, he died. Renee held his hand as he passed. "I was so happy I could be with him at the end," she says.

But this seemingly fractured fairy tale isn't about its sad ending. It's about a hopeful one for anyone in Renee's previous situation. Just as the death of Renee's first husband led to a closer relationship with her brother, and eventually a new beau, Grant's death prompted Renee to have a closer relationship with her son, Marty. The two had drifted away from each other through the years. "We truly bonded," she says, "we truly connected."

As America grays, roughly seventy-eight million baby boomers may be losing some of their "wrinkled" connections with long-time friends, coworkers, church members and, yes, spouses. They also will be finding new connections waiting for them — if they're able to identify them, as Renee was able to do despite her personal reluctance and social comforts as a single woman.

Sociologists say that as these baby boomers begin retirement, many will be seeking new personal connections in their lives — outside of the workplace. Plenty of these hard-charging movers and shakers will feel the need to

Do you blame your parents for missed or unfulfilled relationships? Do you blame your childhood? Your spouse? Your fears?

make amends, or atone, for the disconnecting deeds of their youth, when "earning" an income, "climbing" the corporate ladder, and "chasing" success were first, second, and third priorities.

Taking this notion one step further can lead to the "Scrooge effect" as people age and catch glimpses of their own mortality. The Scrooge effect essentially shows that when we are reminded of death, even in its subtlest of forms we're more likely to seek connections to others.

The phenomenon gets its name from Ebenezer Scrooge, the miserable old miser in Charles Dickens' "A Christmas Carol." It was Scrooge's encounter with the Ghost of Christmas Yet to Come — when he saw his name on a tombstone — that finally swayed his bitter attitude toward others, and of course, toward Christmas.

Social scientists say such a Scrooge effect can also prompt new friendships and new romantic relationships, as well as a newfound appreciation for volunteering and attending church or social functions more often. For many people, it can mean simply showing up at the same coffee shop each morning and being recognized out of a crowd of customers.

However, this Scrooge effect didn't come into play with Tyler, a ten-year-old boy whose Christmas wish came true, all because of connections with other kids his age. Here's Tyler's story.

Tyler got a phone call on a Monday afternoon, during school. His mother was on the line. It was sort of an emergency, she told his teacher. Tyler picked up the phone. The news was bad. His mom's car was just stolen.

The fourth-grader quickly put two and two together and began to cry. The tears weren't about the family's 1994 Buick Century. The lingering sobs were for something much more valuable than a silly car. The tears streamed down for what was in the car's trunk, inside a stuffed Brinks security box.

Tyler asked his teacher if he could go into another room, to be alone, away from other students. There he cried more, thinking of what was stolen from him. Inside that box was Tyler's most prized possession in the whole world.

Remember when your entire world consisted only of your friends, your neighborhood, your collectibles? Remember when you begged, borrowed and saved up for all those Barbie dolls, Matchbox cars, Pogs, or whatever? Remem-

Do you allow work to become a convenient excuse from becoming involved in coveted relationships?

ber when you spent most of your time organizing them, playing with them, or trading them? Well, Tyler knows.

Since kindergarten, Tyler has collected Yu-Gi-Oh trading cards. Packs of them. Boxes of them, gently put into plastic sleeves. Organized. Sorted. Coveted. For almost five long years. Half of his life. Christmas gifts. Birthday gifts. Allowance money.

Tyler figured his collection was valued at $1,200. Sure there were 500 "common" cards, but he also had hundreds of special ones, too. Tyler placed his tidy world in the trunk of his mom's car on a Sunday, to keep it safe until after school on Monday. His mom, Jennifer, drove the car that day to her college classes. When she returned to her car, it wasn't there. It was stolen. She called the cops. Then she called Tyler to arrange his ride home from school. You already know his reaction.

That evening at their home he cried more. Even when his mom bought him two Yu-Gi-Oh booster packs to cheer him up, "he bawled his eyes out," she says. He also became a little fearful, making sure his mom locked their home doors and closed the shades. Police had no clue on the stolen car's whereabouts or who might have stolen it.

At Tyler's age, he might think his collection was taken by an "Archfiend," a special category of Yu-Gi-Oh cards, with an evil name like Axe of Despair, Shadow Tamer, and Beast of Talwar. But, he immediately started his new collection and put up a reward for his old collection.

"I'll give 'em a couple of my best cards," Tyler promised if his collection was found.

After word got out about Tyler's stolen Yu-Gi-Oh collection, the first call came from a young boy. "Hi, this is Aaron. I have some cards for Tyler."

Then the sweetest girl's voice called to say, "Hi, my name is Aanchal. Me and my brother Amijharna want to help Tyler."

The first email arrived soon after. "My name is Dominic and I am thirteen years old. I too collected those cards and … I want to donate my entire collection to (Tyler) but I don't know how."

And this one: "My name is Dakota and I am eleven yrs old. I read the story about Tyler's Yu-Gi-Oh cards being stolen... I have over six hundred fifty cards in good condition to give him that have been sitting on a shelf in my closet. I hope I can give these cards to him by Christmas."

And this one: "I am in 8th grade now, but when I was in around 4th and 5th grade I used to collect them and I really valued them … but this boy needs them more than I do.

Sincerely, Marcella."

More phone calls came in, echoing Aaron's unexpected offer. More emails arrived, similar to Dominic's generous gesture. In all, dozens of kids or their parents rushed into action to help Tyler.

The first box of Yu-Gi-Oh cards arrived the following

Connect your thoughts

morning. Another plastic baggie of cards followed. Then a gift-wrapped box of more cards. In all, children and their parents hand-delivered more than 10,000 cards to Tyler. That's right, 10,000 cards.

Yeah, we know. They're just some silly trading cards we're talking about. Tyler didn't lose his kidney, or his wheelchair, or his siblings. But, still, here are these kids, from six years old to sixteen-years old, asking parents if "it's OK" to give their prized cards to a boy they never met. They didn't need some Scrooge effect to connect with a stranger.

It's not as if they cared whether Tyler lived in their neighborhood or a world away. They gave to give, period. They were invited to bring their gifts for a boy they had never met. They arrived early, carrying boxes, gift bags and plastic baggies of those cards.

Tyler's mother couldn't believe so many kids would part with their cards for her son. They did. She couldn't believe their parents would fight rush-hour, crazy-busy, Christmas shopping traffic for her son. They did.

Some cards came with handwritten letters from kids, like this one from Nick: "Dear Tyler, I know how it feels to lose your cards. I just hope these cards help you."

One bag of cards came from the father of a young boy who had died earlier that year. He wanted Tyler to have his son's collection.

Another box came from a girl who figured she had enough toys and such for Christmas.

"I've never ever seen so many cards," Tyler said to no one in particular.

Tyler's mother watched as the kids surrounded her son, sorting through all the cards. She didn't say much. She couldn't say much. She didn't have to. She just covered her mouth and quietly sobbed, watching her little boy experience the joy of connecting with others. (*To view photos of Tyler with all his cards, visit our Web site at www.connectionsbook.com.*)

As Jennifer discovered first-hand, we can all learn from Tyler and his new "Yu-Gi-Oh friends." Not only did Tyler *tell* others what he wanted (as we suggested in an earlier chapter), but he also had the trust of a child to hope others wouldn't let him down.

They didn't.

Connect your thoughts

Connecting With Others
ACTION ITEMS

The following action steps may help spark your brainstorming process.

1. Listening is a lost art, and too many people insist on always being the colorful paintbrush. Without getting all Zen on you, sometimes it's better to be the blank canvas and simply listen to what others have to say.

2. Your destiny is shaped by *who* you connect with. What you choose to do with those connections determines your life. Write down five people with whom you would like to connect.

3. Which family connections do you want to leave behind for your loved ones? For example:

 a. Memorable vacations?
 b. Acts of kindness or selflessness?
 c. Your legacy?

3. Host a cookout to meet your neighbors.

4. Have you neglected any relationships you cherish? Write down three relationships you've neglected.

5. Instead of texting or emailing, try calling or writing a letter to someone.

6. Have dinner together with your family or friends.

7. Ask your family/friends what they like, and find a way to connect with their suggestions and create a bond.

Who should you contact today to reveal your heartfelt feelings, or invite to spend time together?

Three 'quick tips' to connecting with others

Connecting with others doesn't require an esoteric understanding of the inter-connectedness between everything in the universe, or other such Zen-like teachings.

The fastest and easiest way to begin connecting in any social situation is simpler than you might think. All it takes is a genuine gesture you already perform dozens of times a day, hopefully more.

It's called smiling.

You'd be surprised how many doors can open with the master key of a genuine smile. Remember, it doesn't cost a dime and it takes only 17 muscles, compared to 43 to form a frown. A smile goes a long way to connecting with other people and creating an instant likeability.

A second and often underestimated social connector is eye-to-eye contact. There's no faster way to sabotage a new relationship than by averting your eyes while talking or interacting with someone.

A third "connecting with others" staple is to avoid talking too much, especially about yourself. In our fast-paced, drive-thru, disposable society, everyone always tends to talk, talk, talk. You can usually say more to others by saying less.

Try integrating these three suggestions the next time you connect with others.

*"Life is just one 'aha' moment after another —
the trick is getting to them while you can still
take advantage of those connections."*

— *Anonymous*

Connecting Before It's Too Late

Dale didn't grow up with the usual connections, those that almost everyone else enjoyed as a baby, a child, or an adult. In fact, he barely grew at all.

For decades, Dale's quiet but determined father carried him around in a makeshift carry-cradle. To church, to the store, out to eat — the father didn't mind one bit. Dale was born with a severe form of osteogenesis imperfecta, brittle bone disorder. His tiny, deformed legs dangled uselessly from countless broken and mended bones.

By the time he turned 10 he had already broken his bones hundreds of times. He rarely complained. "He screamed in pain every time we picked him up," his mother says.

Dale's breakable body may have been shortchanged by genetics, or by God, but his spirit wasn't. When Dale came into this world, the doctor told his mother, JoAnn, the flat-out truth about her newborn baby boy: "Something is seriously wrong. Don't expect him to live very long." JoAnn figured right there that she'd take every day the good Lord gave her with her son. She never dreamed she'd get so many days. No one else did, either.

On April 11, 1957, Dale was born by cesarean birth. It's a good thing. A natural birth may have killed him. "Dale was awful fragile," recalls JoAnn, a small woman who also was born with serious health ailments. "So we didn't hold him any more than we had to."

Dale learned how to suck on a bottle alone, lying on his side, never cradled in his mother's bosom like other babies. Even as a first-time mother, JoAnn devised a way to pick up her baby without touching him, by lifting him in a blanket underneath from both sides. Sometimes, just changing his diaper broke his tiny bones. They'd know by either hearing something crack, or watching Dale's face contort in pain and scream out. Casts were out of the question. They were too heavy and his bones would just break again anyway.

When Dale was three months old, a local doctor gave JoAnn advice she took to heart. "Don't treat your child any differently than you would a normal child," he told her. "Wherever you go, he goes."

The Browns did just that. As an infant and toddler, Dale was unable to walk or even sit up, so his father, Donald, carried him around in makeshift baskets, cradles, and strollers. One was made of wood, with metal handles and a bungee cord to keep Dale from falling.

Donald worked for nearly forty years at a local factory. His muscular, tattooed right arm hauled Dale just about everywhere. This carried on for years, then decades.

"We just did what we thought was right, like any parent would do," JoAnn explains. The couple never found the cause of Dale's condition. They never really cared. Their son's breakable body may have been shortchanged, but his intelligence wasn't.

"He had above normal smartness," says Donald, a quiet man who spends words like they're $50 bills. "I was always proud of that." The couple also was proud of Dale's first words — "Mommy" and "Daddy."

At age six, Dale started school, with several different teachers visiting his home daily, teaching him the three Rs through the years. He had trouble holding big text books, but he picked up everything fast. His parents and siblings gave him hand-held games to play, along with crossword puzzles and magazines. He even learned how to crochet. JoAnn still keeps a Dale-crocheted toaster cover and pot holder in her kitchen.

At age nine, Dale celebrated First Communion with other Catholic kids his age. His proud parents still have photos of the public event in August, 1966. As a teenager, Dale stayed mostly at home, in the same rural house his parents still live in. His small bedroom was filled with Peanuts characters, like Snoopy, telling him to "Keep Smiling." He did. Often. His family thought his facial muscles would get sore from all his smiling. They never did.

Connect your thoughts

In 1976, when Dale was nineteen, he planned on graduating high school from his home, his only classroom. When high school officials invited him to take part in the official graduation ceremony in the school gymnasium, it surprised the family, and it surprised Dale, too. Finally, his family figured, Dale would be one of the students. Graduation Day would be a day of normalcy in an otherwise abnormal life.

The Sunday afternoon ceremony began with less pomp and more circumstance when the first graduate's name was called through the public address system — "Dale Francis Brown."

Dale couldn't believe it. Neither could his family. At first, just one fellow graduate rose, then another, then the entire graduating class sprang to its feet in applause. Then every guest, every parent, every teacher stood to applaud. Dale's parents were floored. Their son — who never once stood on his own in his life — received an emotional standing ovation from his peers. "There wasn't a dry eye," says his sister Tammy, who played flute in the school band that afternoon.

Fast-forward thirty years. Donald recalled this special night for his son and he still couldn't keep a dry eye. All he could say was the word "proud." Three times. JoAnn even pulled out Dale's diploma to validate their pride.

After high school, Dale tried learning tax accountancy, but the books were too heavy to lift and his mother's poor health made it hard for her to carry him to college or to a local accountant. At age nineteen, Dale retired to home. The years peeled away. 1980. 1985. 1990. Dale's short body didn't grow length-wise, but he did gain weight, once getting up to 70 pounds.

Lifting him got more difficult, and his parents eventually had to buy him a wheelchair. Later, JoAnn had hip surgery and simply couldn't lift him any more. Donald retired in 1992, yet he still hauled his son into and out of bed, into the bathroom, into the American Legion for bingo, and everywhere else, just as the doctor had suggested decades before.

Dale's little brother, Kerry, defined the fatherly act as "pure determination, nothing less." Tammy notes with awe, "My dad was simply Superman."

Dale eventually found the joys of a home computer, playing video games and sending e-mails to everyone he knew. He celebrated his fortieth birthday at a local American Legion and planned to return there for his fiftieth. He was content and cared for, but something was missing. His freedom. "He wanted to experience life more on his own," says his brother. "He yearned for it," says his sister.

At age forty-six, Dale made the decision to move into an assisted living facility near his home. "We didn't want him

Connect your thoughts

to go, but he made up his mind," JoAnn says flatly. "He felt like he was a burden to us," Donald adds. "But he wasn't. Never was. Not once."

At the center, Dale used a motorized wheelchair to zip around the hallways, a luxury he didn't have inside his small home. He went through two battery chargers while there. His parents visited him daily, usually finding him using the center's computer, or chatting with his all-time favorite nurse and close friend, Lisa.

Lisa was the only nurse Dale trusted to lift him alone. She bought him DVDs on eBay. She went shopping for him to buy Mother's Day gifts. She helped him play bingo, his favorite game. The two emailed each other often. Dale even had her autographed photo on his wall.

There was just something about him," Lisa says. "He was so happy to be alive. He was the sweetest, most compassionate person I ever met. I loved him."

On Dec. 8, 2006, Dale battled a lingering cold. He stayed in bed all day and not once made it to his beloved computer. "Dale, what's wrong?" Lisa asked him. "I think this cold is getting to me," he replied. About 8 p.m., Lisa tucked him in for the night. In the hallway she passed his parents. JoAnn and Donald arrived to make plans for his Christmas homecoming. They too were surprised he was still in bed.

"Dale, what's wrong?" his mother asked. "I'm just tired," Dale replied. His parents tucked him in and said goodbye, thinking he needed a good's night sleep. At 4:30 a.m. the next morning, JoAnn got a phone call.

Dale died in his sleep. No one knew why.

Later, one doctor told the family that Dale's loving heart

was simply too big for his little body. An autopsy was suggested but his parents said no. "He hurt enough during his life," JoAnn reasons. "I don't want him hurting any more."

A steady stream of old friends, former teachers and total strangers attended Dale's funeral. Many echoed the same line: "Thank you for sharing Dale with us." More than one hundred sympathy cards arrived out of nowhere. The family was touched beyond words.

But not Lisa, Dale's favorite nurse. In a long handwritten letter, she wrote, "You were my best friend, my strength and my pride. Only God may know why, but I will get by... I'm sorry I never told you all I wanted to say. Never had I imagined you leaving without just a good-bye." In a memorial service held later at the care center, Donald couldn't keep his emotions under wrap any longer.

"He lost it," JoAnn recalls.

Donald, a proud but deeply hurt man, is still reeling from losing Dale. He misses carrying around his son. "He kept us all together," Donald says.

Before we left JoAnn and Donald's home, where Dale's bedroom is still pretty much intact, we turned to ask one final question. Why? Why did you allow us to write about

Connect your thoughts

your son, despite his disability, his abnormal lifestyle, and all his problems?

"We want the world to know about our son," JoAnn replies. "The world missed who he was and now we miss him, too."

Oddly enough, Dale's obituary in the local newspaper was even shorter than most others. But his impact in those forty-nine years looms tall, very tall. (*To view photos of Dale, visit our Web site at www.connectionsbook.com.*)

After Jerry's column on Dale ran, he was overwhelmed with calls, emails and even handwritten letters from people who knew Dale at some point in his life. He was repeatedly told Dale genuinely touched them, and they felt somehow connected to him — and each other — through his life, and his death.

"He taught me so much," one woman says. "He inspired me," one man recalls.

And on it went for weeks from perfect strangers, or at least people who Dale's family *thought* were perfect strangers. They weren't. Not really. And all because of Dale, the brittle-boned baby who barely grew physically, but nonetheless grew to be connected to oh so many people.

Dale had many seemingly hidden connections, yet his family found out only after he died. This happens all too often with too many people. They think they're not connected to very many people, if anyone at all. It's only after they're gone that their family, friends, and loved ones realize just how connected they were.

If you had one month to live, which connection would you focus on most?

Have you ever attended a funeral for a loved one or friend only to be pleasantly surprised by how many people showed up to pay their respects — simply because they felt connected to the deceased? By then, it's too late for the deceased, isn't it?

This is exactly what happened at a funeral we attended in late 2007 for a teenage boy who committed suicide. Hundreds of mourners pulsed through the Jewish synagogue where the ceremony took place.

"He was a beautiful soul," the rabbi told guests in Yiddish.

In the lobby, stunned parents stood alongside sobbing teenagers as they waited to sign the lengthy guestbook. "I just spoke to him Friday," one teen told another. "I talked to him Saturday," another teen added.

A mother who stood in line summed up the obvious while staring at all the people who attended the boy's funeral. "If only he could have seen all the people he touched in life," she told another mother standing in line.

Exactly. Unfortunately, it was too late for the teenage boy who obviously was more connected to others than he

Connect your thoughts

thought. It's not too late for you. This is the point of this chapter.

We want to remind you that someone's death shouldn't be the time in your life to realize all your connections with family, friends, loved ones, or even those who you mistakenly believe are only acquaintances. Death doesn't necessarily mean all our connections have to die with the deceased.

Jerry learned these lessons first-hand after his father died on Christmas Eve, 1987. Jerry had no idea how many personal connections his father made in life until his funeral, when so many "strangers" appeared out of nowhere to pay their respects.

Since then, Jerry has written open letters to his father, through his columns, nearly every Christmas Eve, to stay somewhat connected to his dad's memory. Every time he writes one, he hears from many people who not only knew his father, but also still feel connected to him.

Here's a sampling of those columns.

Dear Dad, it's been 19 years since you died on that Christmas Eve morning. I just thought I'd write you again this year, update you on some things, if you have the time.

Like I've written before, sometimes it seems like nineteen minutes since we last talked. Other times, it's more like nineteen centuries. For instance, a few days ago I wrote into my daily planner, "Photo of Dad," reminding myself to look for a photograph of you to run with this column. But when I looked at my planner the following day, I forgot whose dad I needed a photo of — a reader's?

A source's? A friend's? Then it hit me, oh, my dad. To be honest, sometimes I forget I ever had a dad. I'm not sure if that says more about me or you.

Call it irony or coincidence but I usually think of you during those moments when my life is as silent as a cemetery; when I'm not busy, busy, busy (remember being so darned busy?) with so many things that don't matter in life. Not really.

And, of course, I always think of you as Christmas Eve approaches. Yep, for two decades now, it's been Santa Claus, Father Time, and you — not quite the Holy Trinity, but close enough for me.

Twenty years is a long time. But then something always sparks memories of you, like AM talk radio, Pall Mall cigarettes, or saxophone music. Or that you hated shirts with collars and how you'd often fold the collars inside. I hate shirts with collars, too. I usually wear T-shirts and sweat shirts, except at work, where I pretend I'm a working professional.

Remember playing pretend as an adult? I see it all the time.

Hey, I'm not sure if you know this, but all the grandkids call you "Papa," and they call Mom "Nana." Yeah, they

Connect your thoughts

take good care of her, and love it when she shares stories about you, again and again. You know, those stories are pretty much all they have of you these days. Still, they have fewer memories of you than I do.

Hey, remember when you and I drove every Saturday morning to buy lottery tickets? Every week you thought you'd scratch off pay dirt and we'd be "set for life, sonny boy," as you'd tell me. Well, it's OK, we're all doing fine without the winnings. My wife, Cherie, and I are doing great. If you remember, I introduced you two in my last letter. We're best friends. Hey, were you and Mom best friends? I don't recall.

As you might know, I wasn't there with you in the hospital when you died on that Christmas Eve morning. Instead I was home getting ready to come to see you. I've always wondered if that was a good thing or a bad thing. The only vivid memory I have from that bittersweet holiday is of me crying in the shower. I'm still not sure if it was from grief or from relief. I thought aging would clear it up but it's only blurred things more.

Still, through the years I've rationalized it as a good thing, with my lingering images of you being alive and not dead; laughing, not moaning; smoking a cigar, not gasping for air. Funny how we spruce-up the past to comfort the present, huh? Or try to make memories all nice and tidy in a corner of our dusty mind.

But, let's face it; there's a thin line between memories and regrets. I often wonder what regrets you had in life, and if they either melted away or multiplied on your death bed.

Twenty years ago, I probably didn't care about all this. It was my loss not to ask, not yours. And I'm not just saying that because you're dead. Things get a little more sketchy every year, but they haven't faded away entirely. In fact, I still keep a photo of you on our refrigerator. In the photo, you're making something to eat in the kitchen. In your robe. I found it fitting. Still do. Don't get a big head. It's on the side of the fridge, not the front.

Also, don't get mad but I haven't been to your grave in quite a while. Heck, I'm still not convinced you're there. Or anywhere except in my head. But when I do visit I always bring cigars. Maybe you've seen them there?

Well, I guess I should go. I'm rambling again. Just wanted you to know I'm thinking of you. Not every day — you know we didn't always get along — but every once in a while. Time has softened me, I guess. How about you?

Been nice talking to you, even if I'm talking only to myself again.

Love, Jerry

P.S. Mom is doing great. We're taking good care of her just as you asked. Oh, and Merry Christmas if that matters where you're at.

Would you, too, tell someone's gravesite your thoughts

Connect your thoughts

and feelings you wouldn't tell them while they were alive?

Just as Dale's connections continued after *his* death — with his family, his friends, his loved ones, and even his acquaintances — the connection between Jerry and his deceased father continues some twenty years later. This illustrates the staying power of certain connections — connections after death.

We're not talking about séances, or the afterlife, or *literally* connecting with the dead. We're talking about those connections that all of us still have with people who have died. How these connections are just as real, just as tangible, just as powerful, as connections with those living in our lives today. These connections often get brushed aside, as if they're not as important to our well-being or future happiness. We all know they are, especially for those of us who've lost a loved one, like Rita, who struggles through "any parent's worst nightmare."

On June 25, 2007, Rita stood over her daughter's body.

Just minutes earlier, a gangster's bullet had pierced the 13-year-old girl's head. Through her sobs, Rita heard her daughter struggle to breathe as police created a barricade around the bloody crime scene.

Through her screams, Rita saw the bullet hole as an ambulance screamed in the distance. Through her shock, Rita saw her daughter's eyes opened but staring blankly, right through her.

"My baby couldn't see me," Rita says through fresh tears, reliving the memory in her mind. "She couldn't see her mother. I'll never forget that look on my baby's face."

This single image has haunted Rita since a gang member emptied his 9-mm handgun into a nearby playground over a turf battle; since Rita's daughter, Schanna, stood at the wrong place at the wrong time; since the college-bound honor student hit the ground near a "Play it safe" playground sign.

Just twenty minutes earlier, Rita had walked past the small neighborhood park — a half-block from the family's apartment — on her way home from the bus stop after work. She gave Schanna a $20 bill to buy herself a slice of watermelon from a street vendor, and told her to bring back the change.

"OK, Ma," Schanna told her mother, flashing that million-dollar smile, "I'll be back."

Those were the last words Schanna spoke to her mother.

Since then, Rita has waded through a wreckage of paren-

Connect your thoughts

tal regrets: What if she hadn't given Schanna money to buy watermelon? What if she had hung around the park a few minutes longer to jump out in front of that wayward bullet? What if she told Schanna to go home with her instead? What if, what if, what if?

Then, maybe Rita's niece wouldn't have bolted into her apartment screaming, "Auntie, auntie, Schanna's been shot in the head!" Then, maybe Rita wouldn't have prayed out loud as she ran to the park: "God, tell me my niece is wrong. Tell me my niece is wrong!" Maybe doctors wouldn't have worked on her brain-dead daughter through the middle of the night until finally calling to say, "Your daughter's heart stopped beating. We're very sorry."

Rita raised Schanna, one of three siblings, to be everything she, herself, wasn't — Schanna was outgoing, open to strangers, always smiling in public. "She was everything I taught her to be, and then some. She was my champion," says Rita, who called her daughter "my lovely" and "pumpkin pie" since she was a child.

In their close-knit urban community, neighbors didn't call Rita "ma'am" or "Rita." They called her "Schanna's mom." Rita took it as high praise. Her daughter attracted strangers' smiles and friends' waves as a playground attracts children, she says. (*To view a photo of Rita and Schanna, visit our Web site at www.connectionsbook.com.*)

Schanna also had her life's plans written in stone: Graduate eighth grade. Enter high school. Play organized basketball. Get an athletic scholarship to college. Attend culinary arts school. Play in the Women's National Basketball Association. Retire to open a restaurant called "Susana," her name in Spanish.

"She had it all planned out," Rita says. "We had it all planned out. And then...."

Gang warfare snuffed out her plans at what should have been a universal safety zone for kids — a school playground. That day, rival gang members stood across from each other amid an invisible dividing line in Shanna's neighborhood. One gang member shot at the other gang member, but missed. Instead, he hit Schanna in the head. She fell instantly.

"They stole my baby," Rita says crying. "It's any parent's worst nightmare."

Rita, a single parent who speaks softly and thoughtfully, visits the playground daily, usually late at night so she can be "alone with Schanna." There, Rita tells Schanna what she normally told her while she was alive, about her work day, her thoughts, her hopes, her dreams.

She also pays weekly visits to Schanna's gravesite, usually on Saturday, taking two buses and a train to see her daughter. There, she quietly sits atop her daughter's grave, speaking to her as if she were alive, playfully hiding behind a tree or a headstone. Schanna never pops her head out, smiling or giggling as she did since she was a

Connect your thoughts

baby.

Here, under the quiet heavens, Rita wonders if she did something wrong to displease God, and if that's why He took Schanna away from her. She wonders about every conceivable scenario that would have saved her daughter's life that night. She wonders what her daughter's high school graduation would have been like. Whom she would have fallen in love with. Her wedding day. Her pregnancies. Her dreams. Everything.

"We will be connected forever," Rita says. "Nothing will ever change that."

This is the power of after-death connections, whether they involve a child, a parent, a relative, a close friend, or especially, a spouse. Do you have such connections? Whether it's been two years or twenty years after someone's death? Have you ever noticed that in certain loving, long-term marriages when one of the spouses passes away, the survivor sometimes dies shortly thereafter? Certain human connections are needed so badly in life that we literally die without them. Other matrimonial survivors, like David, trudge on alone, connected more to fresh memories than to future memorials.

David wrote us just one week after his wife, Audra, died. He wanted to tell the world about his best friend, the love of his life, the most beautiful person in the world, and the mother of his three young girls. He wanted at least one person to read that Audra died of pancreatic cancer at age forty. She didn't know she had it until it was too late. Just one person to read about her life, her smile, her laugh, her hope, her death.

With his three-year-old daughter clutching his leg, he talked for more than an hour at his kitchen table. A photo of Audra peeked over his shoulder from the refrigerator, next to his girls' artwork.

The entire time he was on the verge of tears, painful tears, reluctant tears. But he didn't cry once. Not one tear. He instead spoke about his wife in the present tense —"she's a fighter" — and then paused, catching himself, correcting himself — "she was a fighter."

When driving, he still turns to her in the passenger seat and begins to talk, then catches himself and stops. If he's alone, without the girls, he'll continue his thoughts out loud. He can't help himself.

He's OK during the busy day, making sure his girls are

What legacy do you want to leave behind?

OK. It's the nights that get to him. When the silence suffocates him. When her smiling face pops into his head.

He went from happily watching the Fourth of July parade with his family to being told by a doctor that his wife had two months to live. Two months. How do we squeeze a lifetime of plans and dreams into two months, he wondered.

Near the end, he remembers driving with Audra to the hospital and seeing her yellow jaundiced face in the sunlight. He knew right then and there it wouldn't be long.

At the end, he remembers begging Audra to "let go," and "give in." And assuring her, "the girls will be OK." That was the only time he broke down in front of her. Audra looked at David and told him, "Don't cry, sugar." Those were her last words: "Don't cry, sugar."

Exactly one year after Audra died, we received an email from David. "One year ago today my angel went to heaven," his brief note began. Sure, he was still crushed, bitter, and even angry. But he also told us how he recently honored Audra's death by taking part in a hundred-mile bicycling marathon for cancer research in Philadelphia. After months of training, it was his love for Audra — not his anger or bitterness — that propelled him to its end, despite both knees giving out half-way into the marathon.

During the grueling fundraiser, David repeatedly looked down at his odometer — 50 miles, 60 miles, 70 miles — and repeatedly figured he'd never finish. During those moments, he looked down at a photo of Audra that he had stuck to his bicycle, reminding him why he was there.

"No matter how much pain this is," he told himself while pedaling, "it will never be as much pain as she had." He kept pedaling until the end, just as Audra did in her race against cancer. "It was the most difficult thing I've ever done in my life," he told us.

And he did it with only the *memory* of a connection.

Will people remember you after you're gone?
For what reasons? What deeds?
Which personal connections?

Connecting Before It's Too Late
ACTION ITEMS

The following action steps may assist your brainstorming process.

1. Write down what your childhood dreams were. Reconnect.

2. What legacy do you want to leave behind? Write down what you want stated on your tombstone, or in your eulogy.

3. If you received the news of knowing you had six months to live (versus not knowing), what connections would be most important to you?

4. Write down the top three things you would want your family to remember about you.

5. It's never too late to be who you might have been. Write down the top three connections you need to make, or people you need to reconnect with, before it's too late.

Connect your thoughts

*"I guess I had a 'connection' with
my unborn child without even knowing it."*
— *Sandy*

The Mother-Child Connection

Sandy was stricken with a dire illness at age 5, drastically hampering her life as a young girl — yet dramatically coming to her rescue later in life as a mother. This motherly rescue would also play a major role in the creation of this book. Let us explain.

As a young girl, Sandy suffered through three separate attacks of rheumatic fever, a severe infectious disease characterized by painful swelling and inflammation of the joints, and frequently resulting in permanent damage to the heart.

"I remember during the acute stage of the disease I would run a fever and the joints in my arms were swollen and reddened, causing pain even while lying motionless," Sandy recalled.

To make matters worse, she also had the typical childhood ailments like the mumps, measles, chickenpox, and whooping cough.

For each attack, the first striking her in the late 1940s, doctors prescribed up to a year of bed rest. During the acute stage of the disease, she was completely bedridden and couldn't even get up to use the bathroom.

Of course, this also meant no public school for young Sandy, and teachers instead visited her home with lessons and homework.

"During my grade school years I was home-schooled with two wonderful teachers, Mrs. Grecco and Mrs. Edmundson," Sandy said. "They came two to three times a week with their lessons, leaving homework each time when I was well enough to complete it."

Sandy remembers looking forward to her younger sister coming home from school and sharing her classes and friendships with her. During this time, nurses frequently stopped by to draw her blood. Yet she also has fond memories of spending hours making beautiful jewelry from shells her mother bought her as gifts. Also developing a deep loving relationship with her maternal grandmother, Grandma Cook, who lived with the family and made Sandy her favorite.

Grandma Cook emigrated alone from Lithuania at age 16 to live with her aunt and uncle in Chicago. Following custom from the old country, the couple arranged for their niece's marriage to a Lithuanian man several years her senior. She eventually grew to love the stranger turned husband and they had four children together, with Sandy's mother being the youngest.

Grandma Cook, Sandy recalled, "was the first connection in my life."

This first connection helped nurture Sandy as she recovered from rheumatic fever. The two would listen to old radio shows together, make shell jewelry, and develop a tight bond.

In time, as Sandy improved, she visited doctors' offices for various tests, including an old-fashioned fluoroscopy procedure to show the health of her beating heart. More importantly, she recalls one older doctor telling her to get her rest so she could one day be strong enough to have children.

With this in mind, Sandy was never allowed to run, ride a bike or take part in gym classes when she finally returned to school. This further separated Sandy from her classmates, even into high school, and only made her more quiet and introverted. She joined the Glee Club and even received an award for earning the highest grades over her four-year high school career.

Two years after graduation, she met and fell in love with Ron, a Purdue University-educated engineer who, in fact, taught Sandy how to ride her first bike. The couple had two children without thinking twice about Sandy's childhood illnesses.

However, the couple's third pregnancy was more of a problem. After trying for months without any luck, doctors told the couple not to see a fertility expert until they were

Connect your thoughts

unsuccessful for one year. Almost to the day, they finally conceived. But more problems awaited them.

Sandy's blood was RH negative, Ron's was RH positive, and that posed a problem for their third pregnancy and third child. Sandy became sensitized by the RH positive blood of her first child, a daughter. Due to RH antibodies produced in her blood from that pregnancy, the risky condition could result in a hemolytic disease for her fetus, characterized by anemia, jaundice, enlargement of the liver and spleen, generalized edema and even possible death.

Since this took place in the 1970s, the doctors' medical equipment, testing and procedures weren't as sophisticated as they are today. Plus, a mother-to-be couldn't learn the sex of her child since ultrasounds didn't exist. The only way doctors could check what was going on inside her womb was with a needle biopsy of the amniotic fluid — while strategically avoiding the growing fetus when they inserted the needle.

During the eighth month of Sandy's pregnancy, two obstetricians and three pediatricians agreed to induce labor. After Sandy was on an I.V. drip for two days without any luck, the doctors decided Sandy should return home, since her baby probably wasn't large enough to be born at that stage anyway. Sandy said no.

"No? Who says no to a team of expert doctors?" they countered.

You have to keep in mind that during this era — before the Internet's wealth of health information and before second guessing physicians became standard procedure for patients -- doctors were treated like gods and patients rarely went against their orders.

Sandy stood her ground, insisting that she deliver her third baby through a C-section, an unusual procedure at the time. Eight months pregnant and with two little ones at home, Sandy argued with doctors and flatly told them she wasn't leaving the hospital. As a compromise, Sandy's doctors said they would take one more blood test and abide by what it showed. Sandy agreed. Fair enough.

Lo and behold, the last blood test proved Sandy correct, and doctors decided to perform a C-section the next morning. She gave birth to a 7-pound, 10-ounce baby boy, but he came into this world with several health problems, including jaundice, a yellow discoloration of the skin.

Doctors later told her if she had returned home to wait longer, her baby probably would not have lived. "Perhaps my being sick as a child made me more aware of my feelings and determination to have my baby," Sandy said in hindsight.

Her baby ended up having multiple and complete blood exchanges, each performed through his navel, plus additional blood transfusions.

"His feet, hands, and temples looked like pin cushions," Sandy recalled.

Connect your thoughts

Making matters worse, her baby needed 0-negative blood and there was a shortage of it in the Kentucky area, where they lived. Ron, Sandy's husband, arranged for coworkers to come into the hospital to donate the needed blood. Sandy's baby stayed in the hospital longer than she did. The young couple was forced to return home without him.

Finally, after their baby was allowed to leave the hospital, the young family visited a neighbor's home for light-hearted socializing and friendly badminton, a needed reprieve from such life and death medical decisions. Their sickly newborn, now 2 months old, slept in a portable carry-on bed in the backyard while his parents chatted and older siblings played with friends.

At one point, the neighborhood children began quarreling, and Sandy went to check her baby to make sure he was still asleep. But the situation was much more dangerous than Sandy thought. Her baby wasn't just restless. He wasn't breathing.

Sandy turned her baby over and he was limp. Blood had clotted from his nose to his mouth. The couple rushed him to the hospital, where the pediatrician who helped deliver him waited. The couple rushed their lifeless baby into the emergency room, and doctors hurriedly worked on him. Minutes later, Sandy heard a throaty scream that sounded like a wild animal's. Her baby boy was revived, but not before acidosis set in, a blood condition often preceding death.

Countless tests were conducted. No results were found. Doctors explained what happened as an aborted crib death. In other words, the baby never should have made it. They also reasoned the baby might have permanent brain damage after going so long without oxygen.

It turns out they were wrong. Again. The baby's health slowly improved through the years. He played like other children and eventually went on to graduate college with a degree in engineering, like his big brother, and his father.

In time, Sandy raised her three children and, after they found lives and careers of their own, so did she. She became a registered nurse in her late 40s. Surely those early childhood, bed-bound connections with encouraging doctors and nurturing nurses played a role in her late-arriving career. And surely so did Grandma Cook, her first connection in life.

But what about her sickly third-born child, you may ask, the little tyke who struggled so mightily to enter this world?

"I guess I had a 'connection' with my unborn child without even knowing it," Sandy said.

But she knows it now, after being reminded about the importance of connections — remember, from *womb* to tomb. The child became a husband, a father of four, and a prestigious partner in a successful engineering firm in Las Vegas. Oh, and he also grew up to co-author this book.

His name is Dennis Berlien.

Connect your thoughts

Connection Coincidences:
'IN 2008, PEOPLE WANT TO CONNECT'

In March, 2006, Jerry sat in a hotel room in Los Angeles, just outside of Universal Studios. The weather was chilly, rainy, and about 55 degrees. The locals there were bundled up in coats, hats and gloves. This vacationer from the Chicago region, where 55 degrees in early March is T-shirt and shorts weather, was amused.

Earlier in the day, he strolled through Universal Studios' CityWalk, a glitzy, flashy, shameless display of commercialism for tourists. It had all the trendy stores, eateries and entertainment venues, from Hard Rock Cafe to Cinnabon to Abercrombie & Fitch.

His entire three-day stay he flirted with random entries, chapters and anecdotes for this book. But for some reason he delayed writing. Maybe it was because he feared he was wasting his time, thinking that this book was a pipe dream that would never materialize. Maybe he feared it *would* materialize.

Remember, some people are more afraid of success than failure; it's a strange bedfellow whose face is often shadowed by either guilt, pessimism, or both. Maybe Jerry was no different.

But then, on the last day of his visit, while Jerry walked past a CityWalk kiosk for some new high-tech gadgetry, a vendor asked him, "Wanna get connected?"

"What?!" Jerry asked, stunned by the coincidence of his offer.

"Don't you want to get connected?" the man repeated matter-of-factly, as if he knew what Jerry was writing about in his hotel room.

Getting "connected," the vendor quickly explained, involved some new video game he was hawking. After pausing to digest his odd query, Jerry passed on the video game offer, but nearly passed out on his offer to "get connected" and the synchronicity of his timing and wording.

Needless to say, Jerry stayed up until 3 a.m. that night working on this book.

Then, in December, 2007, Jerry traveled to Las Vegas to meet with Dennis and put the finishing touches on this book. During his return flight on New Year's Day, he took a break from writing a chapter and opened up a USA Today newspaper.

He glanced at its Life section. Its centerpiece story boldly stated: "**IN 2008, PEOPLE WANT TO CONNECT**." (*Go ahead, look it up — Dec. 31, 2007 edition.*)

Minutes later, the pilot's voice boomed across the plane's loud speaker: "OK, I know you all have *connections*," referring, of course, to the passengers' connecting flights at Midway Airport in Chicago.

Was the pilot's interruption simply a fluke? Was the vendor's exchange in L.A. a chance encounter? Was the USA Today headline merely a coincidence? Of course.

But it was a *timely* coincidence, fluke, and chance encounter. Ones with special meanings to Jerry, which we call "synchronicity" (defined as "events that appear to be connected but have no demonstrable causal relationship").

The trick was that Jerry had to be open to it. He had to be aware of it. He had to make use of it. And he did. So can you.

Remember to be open to your coincidences, your synchronicities, your connections — whatever you want to label them. Even if they come from odd or unlikely places in our seemingly unconnected society.

*"When we get too caught up
in the busyness of the world, we lose
connection with one another — and ourselves."*
— *Jack Kornfield,*
spiritual teacher, author

Epilogue:
Your Connections

We met through the kind of connection you can't always see, at least at first. Somehow it sees you — and eventually transforms you. Some call this luck or coincidence. Others call it fate or synchronicity. We call this particular connection a surprising come-from-behind Chicago Cubs victory over the New York Yankees at Wrigley Field in June, 2003, when Roger Clemens tried to notch his milestone 300th victory.

You see, Dennis is a huge Boston Red Sox fan, even naming his first-born son Boston, where Clemens became famous in the baseball world. Jerry is a die-hard Cubs fan, hoping that his lovable losers could somehow thwart Clemens' attempt for pitching immortality. Dennis came from Nevada for the game. Jerry came from Indiana.

The crowd noise was deafening that day as Clemens pitched his way toward a possible 1 - 0 victory. In the 7th inning, he left the mound for a relief pitcher as his 300th win was being penciled into the history books by Dennis and thousands of obnoxious Yankee fans in the crowd.

But the Yankees' relief pitcher (Juan Acevedo, for you baseball purists) gave up a first-pitch homerun ball to the Cubs batter (Eric Karros, for you Cubbies fans) and Clemens' hopes were dashed by a score of 3 to 1.

We arrived at the ballpark that day with opposing hopes, but after nearly two decades apart from each other, we left with a renewed promise to keep in touch. And we did. Months later, we met again to share the first conversation that reconnected our lives and ultimately created this book.

At the time, we didn't realize this seemingly random connection would change our lives. The realization came only later. Hopefully, with help from this book, the realization of connections in *your* life will come much sooner than ours.

Now that you are more aware of their meaning, their significance, and their elusiveness, you will begin to notice them from this day forward. This is not schmaltzy marketing. This is scientific fact. To explain it, consider the connective powers of the "reticular activator," the part of your brain which instantly and automatically begins noticing things once you are made aware of them.

For example, have you ever purchased a new car and then suddenly began seeing them everywhere on the road? Or have you ever learned that a close friend found a job as a construction worker and then suddenly became more aware of construction workers in your daily routine?

This is how your reticular activator works. And this is

how you will begin to see more and more connections in your daily routine.

Since we began identifying such things, in 2004, we also learned that everyone has a few "moments by which to matter," best defined by best-selling author Robert Kurson.

In the fall of 2008, Kurson lurked in the shadows of a meeting room inside a public library. The award-winning author and gifted wordsmith waited to speak to dozens of fans who showed up to now *hear* his words, too.

Kurson began his writing career as a features reporter for the Chicago Sun-Times, then branched into magazine work before penning two best-seller books, "Shadow Divers" and "Crashing Through."

Kurson quietly took a seat in front of the audience and disappeared in his work, his books, and stories of how he got to where he is today. He earned a philosophy degree from the University of Wisconsin, and another degree from Harvard Law School, before practicing real estate law and installing window blinds to make ends meet.

When he told family and friends he instead wanted to be a writer, they questioned his credibility, saying he didn't write enough, he didn't read enough, and he didn't take any classes to do so.

And they were right, he admits. But he had something more important on his side. His father, he says proudly, was "the single-best master storyteller."

"It must have seeped into my pores," he tells the crowd.

Kurson's 2004 book "Shadow Divers" chronicles the aquatic quest for historical discoveries by single-minded deep-sea divers John Chatterton and Richie Kohler.

The two foes-turned-friends became obsessed with a sunken German U-boat, 60 miles off the coast of New Jersey in the frigid depths of the Atlantic Ocean. The World War II vessel still housed the remains of its nameless crew.

Kurson not only documented the men's quest, but also *why* they risked everything for it. Their marriages, their reputations, even their lives. Both men agreed that their quest became "a moment by which to matter."

It was their chance to do something special, something beautiful, and something true to themselves. Nothing else mattered. And nothing else should.

As such chances go, "some of us get it only once in our life if we're lucky," Kurson explains.

Not only did Chatterton and Kohler seize this once-in-a-lifetime opportunity in their lives, so did Kurson in his life, by diving into writing as a livelihood.

"This is when I felt my first real *connection* with both of them," Kurson says.

This connection would not only bind him to Chatterton and Kohler, but also to the realization that their legacies would hinge on their underwater obsession. For Kurson, his legacy would most likely hinge on his writing.

"What we do now," the divers told Kurson, "is who we will be forever."

With this in mind, what are you doing in life that may define who you are forever?

Maybe now is the time to find your sunken U-boat, figuratively speaking, to ponder the depths of its meaning, and to salvage your "moments by which to matter."

Since you first cracked open this book, have you been

pondering *your* connections in life? Did we spark more connections than missed connections in your past? Did they profoundly change your life? Did you think of someone you've long forgotten? Are you planning on reconnecting with someone?

Ah, questions, questions, questions. As we told you, it's about asking questions. Go ahead and ask yourself the same questions we first asked ourselves in 2004: Am I connected? Am I connected enough? If so, who was my most crucial connection? If not, why not?

If you get stumped, just remember what we've been telling you since page one: "*Everyone* happens for a reason" in your life.

This book isn't strictly our attempt to share with you what we've learned these past several years, and how it may also help you. It's also our way to connect with you. We want to hear from you. Have any of our personal stories resonated with you or your life? Did anyone else's story ring a bell for you? Have they sparked change in you, or possibly renewed hope in our often hopeless world? Do you now recall missed connections in your past, and possible connections in your future?

Regardless if your connections trigger memories of happiness and success, or regrets of bitterness and failure, we want to hear your stories for our next book, already in progress. We're writing a follow up book about all the connections we couldn't fit into this book, and we want to include more stories from new readers like you. We want "*Connections*" to continue as a dialogue, not a monologue.

The fastest way to contact us is to visit our Web site,

www.connectionsbook.com, and fill out our online questionnaire. Feel free to write as many details as you want, and don't forget to include your contact info. If you're not a regular surfer in cyberspace, you can snail mail us your story to Connections Book, P.O. Box 649, Portage, In. 46368.

Our Web site also includes ongoing updates regarding our next book, an interactive blog to continue this dialogue, a newsletter to share **new** *Connections* stories with you, and bonus questions to help identify and develop *your* connections, and maybe even publish them.

The site also includes photographs of many of the people featured in this book, and information on future *Connections* seminars, workshops, and lectures for interested groups and corporations.

One last time, are you connected? Of course you are.

About the Authors

JERRY DAVICH has written thousands of stories, columns and feature projects for various publications across the country, including newspapers, magazines, and health journals.

He began his writing career as a political cartoonist before realizing his passion for narrative storytelling — from following a high school student with disabilities to her first prom, or chronicling the immediate aftermath of the Sept. 11, 2001 terrorist attacks in New York City, to watching an elderly woman with terminal cancer slowly die in a hospice, and jumping out of a skydiving plane with a microphone in hand.

Jerry has covered several news beats — including health, environment, features and social issues, to name a few — but his emphasis is always the same: To profile ordinary people — their hopes and dreams, joys and pitfalls — and the often extraordinary connections in their lives.

He never planned on writing this book until experiencing a serendipitous series of his own connections and missed connections. Today, he's the metro columnist for the Post-Tribune Newspaper in Northwest Indiana, as well as a freelance writer for several national publications and, now, a book author.

Jerry lives in Portage, Indiana, with his wife, Cherie, and has two adult children.

DENNIS BERLIEN is a husband, and father of four children who reside in Las Vegas, Nevada. He enjoys spending quality time with his family near Newport Beach, California.

He enjoys playing competitive tennis and basketball, studying jiu-jitsu combat training, and he recently completed the Honolulu Marathon with his father in Hawaii.

A Leadership in Energy and Environmental Design (LEED) accredited professional, he received his Bachelor of Science in Electrical Engineering from North Carolina State University. With over 15 years of professional experience, Dennis excels in overseeing engineering services including sustainable design and LEED certified buildings.

He currently serves as a principal for a Boston, Massachusetts-based engineering firm and manages its West Coast operations. He is also responsible for building and maintaining relationships with developers, owners, and architects.

As co-author of "Connections," Dennis aspires to offer consulting services based on the theme of this book. He considers his persistence, ability to adapt to change and, just as importantly — his personal connections — as the keys to his success.

Connect your thoughts

Connect your thoughts